THE AMATEUR RADIO ASTRONOMER'S HANDBOOK

THE AMATEUR RADIO ASTRONOMER'S HANDBOOK

JOHN POTTER SHIELDS

ILLUSTRATIONS BY RICHARD AND DEBORAH WAXBERG

Crown Publishers, Inc.
New York

Copyright © 1986 by John Potter Shields

All rights reserved.
No part of this book may be reproduced or transmitted
in any form or by any means, electronic or mechanical,
including photocopying, recording, or by any
information storage and retrieval system, without permission
in writing from the publisher.

Published by Crown Publishers, Inc.,
225 Park Avenue South, New York, New York 10003,
and represented in Canada by
the Canadian MANDA Group

CROWN is a trademark of Crown Publishers, Inc.

Manufactured in the United States of America

Library of Congress Cataloging-in-Publication Data
Shields, John Potter.
   The amateur radio astronomer's handbook.
   Includes index.
   1. Radio astronomy—Popular works. I. Title.
QB477.S45 1986   522'.682   86-6375
ISBN 0-517-55810-6

First Edition

To my father, who encouraged my interest in radio during my childhood and who helped to make this book possible

Contents

	Introduction	1
1.	Comparison of Optical and Radio Astronomy	5
2.	Radio Wave Propagation and the Ionosphere	9
3.	Extraterrestrial Radio Sources	13
4.	Some Optical Astronomy Basics	19
5.	Some Basic Electronics	27
6.	Basic Radio Astronomy Systems	41
7.	The Radio Telescope Antenna	51
8.	Radio Telescope Receivers	61
9.	And Now into Practice	67
10.	Antenna Design and Construction	73
11.	Observing the Sun	79
12.	A 400-MHz Interferometer	85
13.	Receiving Signals from Jupiter	87
14.	Detection of Meteors and Meteor Showers	91
15.	Some Final Words	95
	Index	101

THE JANSKY ANTENNA (*Courtesy Bell Labs*)

Introduction

Like many great discoveries, the science of radio astronomy was born almost by accident. In 1931, a radio engineer by the name of Karl Jansky, an employee of Bell Telephone Laboratories, was assigned the task of determining the cause of electrical interference on transoceanic radio transmissions.

To determine the cause of this interference, Jansky assembled a large steerable radio antenna. The antenna was about 100 feet long and 12 feet high and was mounted on wheels placed on a circular track. The whole arrangement could be rotated through 360 degrees in a horizontal plane so as to survey the whole sky.

With his antenna, Jansky was able to identify three basic types of radio signal interference—local thunderstorms, distant thunderstorms, and interference of an unknown origin. After further investigation, Jansky concluded that this third type of interference was extraterrestrial in origin and appeared to be centered in the region of the Milky Way.

Not much further progress occurred until 1937, when a radio amateur by the name of Grote Reber became interested in Jansky's research. Using only his own funds, Reber assembled a 30-foot parabolic antenna in his backyard. The antenna was designed for operation at about 3,000 megahertz (MHz). (*Hertz* is the new internationally accepted term for the previously used "cycles per second.")

Reber's initial observations with this antenna proved fruitless, so he modified his equipment for operation at the much lower frequency of 150 MHz. At this lower frequency, he was able to detect strong signals from the center of our galaxy. Reber was the first to publish a basic radio signal map of the sky. He was also the first to discover radio signal emission from the sun.

Following World War II, the field of radio astronomy began to expand rapidly. Much of this was due to the development of VHF and UHF receiving equipment for the military during the war. In particular, the development of radar, with its UHF receiver and antenna technology, made possible greatly improved radio telescope systems.

In 1946, the University of Manchester in England constructed a 218-foot parabolic radio telescope. Later this same university built a fully steerable 250-foot telescope. Also in 1946, J. W. Phillips, J. S. Hey, and S. J. Parsons in England began a detailed survey of the radio sky at a frequency of 250 MHz.

Another significant radio telescope installation during this period was the construction of the 250-foot dish antenna at Jodrell Bank in England. Still another important development was the Cross interferometer radio telescope, which was invented by B. T. Mills at Sydney University in Australia.

In March 1951, Ewen and Purcell at Harvard University detected extraterrestrial hydrogen line emissions at 1,420 MHz, using a newly developed UHF radio telescope. Shortly thereafter, this same hydrogen line was identified by Muller and Oort at Leiden, Holland, and by Christianson at Sydney, Australia.

In the United States and Puerto Rico, there are many professional radio telescope installations under the direction of a number of organizations, including Cornell University, the National Astronomy and Ionospheric Center, the National Radio Astronomy Observatory, and the Department of the Navy.

The largest U.S. radio telescope is the VLA (Very Large Array) interferometer located in Socorro, New Mexico. It is capable of providing a resolution, or image sharpness, rivaling that of an optical telescope. This installation consists of 27 individual antennas arranged along three radial arms forming a Y-shaped array. Two of these arms are 13 miles long and the third is 11.6 miles long. A double set of railroad tracks carries a specially designed transporter that moves the antennas to and from the 72 observing stations. The assembly of the system is such that the array can track a radio source across the sky to within 15 seconds of arc.

The second largest radio telescope installation is located in Arecibo, Puerto Rico, and is operated by Cornell University in cooperation with the National Science Foundation. The heart of the Arecibo telescope is the 1,000-foot reflector built in a natural limestone crater. The reflective surface has an area of 24 acres and consists of over 38,000 individual aluminum panels. A platform that serves as a supporting structure for the receiving equipment is suspended by cable over the center of the reflector from three concrete towers.

A unique feature of this installation is that it can be used "in reverse," serving as a powerful radar system. In this mode of operation, it transmits powerful radio signals into the cosmos in the hope of contacting distant civilizations.

Another major radio telescope installation is operated under the direction of the Naval Research Laboratory of the Department of the Navy. The laboratory now operates the Maryland Point Observatory, which consists of an 85-foot parabolic antenna designed for operation at frequencies as high as 50 GHz and an 84-foot antenna designed for frequencies as high as 2 GHz.

The observatory is actively engaged in research in interstellar spectroscopy and very long baseline (VLBL) studies of galactic and extragalactic radio sources.

Another major U.S. radio telescope installation is located in Green Bank, West Virginia, and is operated under the sponsorship of the National Science Foundation. This installation includes a 140-foot telescope, a 300-foot telescope, and an interferometer telescope.

A number of American universities also have radio telescope installations. Perhaps the best known is the antenna operated at Ohio State University.

In addition to the U.S. radio astronomy observatories just mentioned, there are many foreign observatories. In fact, almost every major nation has at least one radio telescope in operation.

Among the larger foreign installations are the Jodrell Bank radio telescopes in Great Britain. These were among the earliest constructed, and they contributed much basic information on galactic and extragalactic radio emissions. Another major radio telescope installation is located in Narrari, Australia. This telescope is unique in that its primary purpose is to investigate solar radio signals. Another major radio telescope installation is located at the Itopatinga Radio Observatory at São Paulo, Brazil. It carries on a wide variety of observations, including low-frequency ionospheric studies of solar radio emissions and centimeter-wavelength radio signal observations.

The table opposite gives a chronological list of the major events in radio astronomy.

The Major Events of Radio Astronomy

1932 Karl Jansky announces the discovery of radio emission from the center of the Milky Way galaxy.

1940 Grote Reber maps the sky at 160 MHz.

1942 Radio waves from the sun are detected independently in England and the United States.

1945 Radio emission from the moon is first detected.

1948 The 10 strongest cosmic radio sources are known.

1949 The Crab nebula, a 900-year-old remnant of a supernova explosion, and two galaxies are identified with cosmic radio sources.

1951 The emission line of neutral hydrogen is detected from interstellar gas.

1953 Cygnus A is found to be a double radio source, the archetypal radio galaxy.

1955 The first planet is detected, radio bursts from Jupiter.

1963 Quasars are discovered by the identification of 3C 273 with a distant starlike object.

1964 Microwave background radiation is discovered, a remnant from the beginning of the universe.

1965 Radio emission from interstellar maser is discovered.

1967 Precisely periodic radio emission leads to the discovery of pulsars.

1967 The first Very Long Baseline Interferometer (VLBI) experiments lead to an improvement in resolution by a factor of more than 100.

1973 The first radio red shifts of a distant quasar are measured.

1974 The most precise measurement of the bending of electromagnetic waves by the sun is made with a radio interferometer and gives a new confirmation of Einstein's theory of general relativity.

1981 Completion of the Very Large Array (VLA), the first truly image-forming radio telescope with an angular resolution better than any optical telescope.

Courtesy of the National Radio Astronomy Observatory.

1 Comparison of Optical and Radio Astronomy

We are going to examine the similarities and differences between optical and radio astronomy. Radio astronomy doesn't compete with optical astronomy; rather, it provides us with observations unattainable by optical methods. There are many thousands of galactic objects that are invisible to the optical telescope but that emit very strong radio signals. Radio astronomy is also a "foul-weather friend," working in rain and shine, night and day.

FREQUENCY AND WAVELENGTH

Let us take a moment to review the definitions of frequency and wavelength. All types of electromagnetic radiation, whether we are talking about radio waves, infrared, visible light, or X-rays, have a certain wavelength and a corresponding frequency. When the frequency goes up, the wavelength becomes shorter. The relationship can be expressed as follows:

$$\lambda = \frac{300,000,000}{f}$$

where: λ = wavelength in meters
300,000,000 = speed of light in meters per second
f = frequency in hertz (cycles per second)

A more convenient arrangement is to convert hertz to megahertz (MHz). The formula is then given as:

$$\lambda = \frac{300}{f \, (\text{MHz})}$$

To see how this formula works, let us take an example. Solving for the wavelength (λ) of 2 MHz, we find that:

$$\lambda = \frac{300}{2} = 150 \text{ meters}$$

Similarly, if we want to find the wavelength of 150 MHz, it will be:

$$\lambda = \frac{300}{150} = 2 \text{ meters}$$

From these examples, you can see that as the frequency goes up, the wavelength becomes shorter.

The entire electromagnetic spectrum extends from the very low frequency end, with wavelengths in the thousands of meters, to the gamma-ray range, with wavelengths measured in thousandths of microns. (A micron is equal to one millionth of a meter.) Starting at the low-frequency end of the electromagnetic spectrum, radio waves with wavelengths from 10,000 meters (30 KHz) to 3,000 meters (100 KHz) define the VLF (very low frequency) range. This range is used by the military for long-range communications, and there are a number of radio navigation beacons in this range. There are several reasons for the choice of this VLF wavelength. Perhaps the most important is that the signal is not energetic enough to penetrate the earth's ionosphere, as are shorter wavelengths, but instead curves around the earth's surface. As a result, it can provide reliable long-distance communication without fading or losing signal strength. Second, these VLF wavelengths can penetrate water and thus are used by the navy for long-distance land-to-submarine communications.

Moving upward, we reach the 100–500 KHz frequency range, which is also used by marine navigation and various types of radio beacons. (Incidentally, 500 MHz is the international low-frequency distress signal.) Next in line is the standard AM broadcast band, 550–1600 KHz (550–180 meters). Moving still upward, we find the shortwave broadcast bands ranging from about 2 MHz to 30 MHz (80–10 meters). Next is the range between 30 MHz

THE ELECTROMAGNETIC SPECTRUM

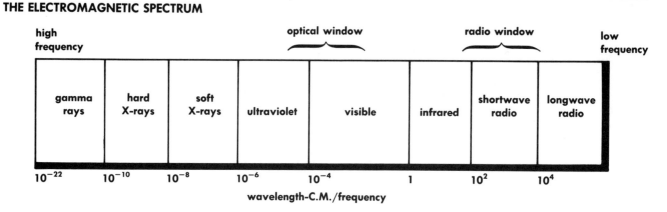

and 300 MHz, which is loosely referred to as the VHF band (10 meters to 1 meter). Notice one important fact—as the *frequency* becomes *higher*, the *wavelength* (measured in meters) becomes *shorter*. This is a fundamental fact that you should keep in mind.

Moving still higher in frequency, we reach the gigahertz (1,000–50,000 MHz) region. Since the wavelengths are progressively shorter, we now measure them in centimeters. (One meter equals 100 centimeters.)

In the frequency ranges that we have just described lies the *radio window*. More specifically, the low end of the radio window is about 18 KHz. Below this frequency, ionospheric absorption severely limits the passage of extraterrestrial signals to the earth.

The upper frequency limit of the radio window is the result of water vapor and CO_2 particles suspended in the atmosphere. The suspended water and CO_2 molecules absorb the microwave energy and convert it into heat. The effect is analogous to a glass of water absorbing energy in a microwave oven.

The wavelengths between the upper end of the radio window and the visible-light region is known as the *infrared band*. These wavelengths are very familiar to us as heat radiation. Every object at a temperature above absolute zero emits infrared wavelengths—the higher the temperature, the greater infrared radiation emitted. Infrared emission is exploited in heat-seeking missiles, heat-sensitive alarm systems, and infrared astronomy.

Up to this point, we have been measuring wavelengths in meters and centimeters. When we are in the infrared range, we use microns. (One micron equals one millionth of a meter.) Here again, note that as the frequency goes up, the wavelength becomes shorter.

Next we come to the *optical window*, which of course we are all familiar with, as this is the area of optical astronomy. We also call it the *visible spectrum*. The longer wavelengths are near the red region, while the shorter wavelengths lie in the violet area of the spectrum.

Moving still further up the spectrum, we come to the ultraviolet range. We are familiar with ultraviolet because, among other things, it gives us that nice suntan. Certain specialized types of astronomy employ UV to detect specific extraterrestrial radiation.

"Soft" and "hard" X-rays occupy the next spot on the frequency spectrum. Soft X-rays do not have the penetrating power of hard X-rays, and they have a longer wavelength. Finally, we come to the shortest wavelength of the spectrum, gamma radiation, which has extremely high energy levels.

Earlier we stated that as the frequency of a signal increases, its wavelength decreases. There is another basic principle in electromagnetic radiation: As the wavelength becomes shorter, its energy becomes greater. What this means is that ultraviolet radiation has more energy than infrared radiation, and similarly, infrared radiation has more energy than radio frequency microwaves.

An interesting example of these differing energy levels can be experienced when you are on the beach. As you bask in the warm sun, you may believe that all that nice heat is giving you that fine tan. Not so! What you are feeling is the infrared energy from the sun, which strikes the outer surface of your skin, causing it to feel warm. You can't see infrared energy; you can only note its effect of heating your skin. What causes the suntan is the much higher energy ultraviolet radiation from the sun. Because of its higher energy level (remember, we said that UV has a higher energy level than IR), the ultraviolet radiation has enough energy to pass through the outer layer of your skin, where it strikes the pigment, causing it to darken.

When you have an X-ray taken, the X-rays pass right through skin and tissues to reveal the bone. Here again, this is possible because of the higher energy levels of X-rays as compared to ultraviolet radiation.

It is interesting to note that X-ray astronomy is now becoming a significant tool. Many cosmic objects emit a tremendous amount of X-ray energy, and this technology is becoming a viable new branch of astronomy.

COMPARISON OF OPTICAL AND RADIO TELESCOPES

There are several basic similarities between optical and radio telescopes. They both serve the same basic purpose, to gather information from an extraterrestrial source and convert it to a measurable quantity. They both have means to collect radiated signals. These gathered signals must be amplified many times, and some device must be provided to interpret the information.

Let us take a look at the accompanying illustra-

COMPARISON OF OPTICAL AND RADIO TELESCOPES

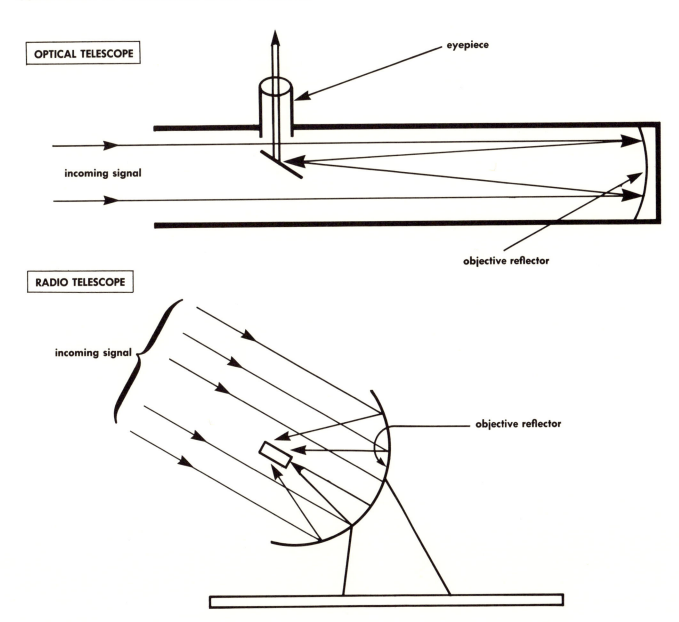

tion, which shows the familiar reflector-type optical telescope. In this case, the extraterrestrial signals to be observed are in the optical wavelengths. The light image is focused on the primary gathering mirror at the rear of the telescope tube. This is analogous to the large antenna surface of the radio telescope.

The larger the optical telescope's primary mirror, the greater its light-gathering ability, and by the same token, the larger the radio telescope's antenna, the greater its radio signal-gathering ability.

The lens in the eyepiece amplifies the image received by the primary mirror in the optical telescope. When the size of the eyepiece changes, so does the amount of optical magnification. In the case of the radio telescope, the signal obtained from the gathering antenna is amplified electronically. Thus, the electronic amplifier in the radio telescope is analogous to the optical telescope's eyepiece.

With the optical telescope, the gathered and amplified light signals are either interpreted visually or recorded on photographic film. In the case of the radio telescope, the readout device may be either a strip chart recorder, an aural device like the speaker of a radio set, or a computer graphics system, which allows in-depth analysis.

Comparative Size

As you have probably noticed, optical telescopes are much smaller than their radio counterparts. The reason for this is the wavelengths involved. As we mentioned earlier, light waves are much shorter than radio waves. Radio wavelengths are measured in meters, while light wavelengths are measured in microns (millionths of a meter). It is a fundamental fact that the size of the signal-gathering system, whether a glass lens or mirrored reflector for an optical telescope or an antenna for a radio telescope, is directly proportional to the received wavelength. Thus, the optical telescope can have a much smaller signal-gathering system than the radio telescope for comparable signal-gathering ability.

Since the radio telescope must have a much larger signal-gathering system, a number of different methods have been devised to increase the effective antenna size. One of the most common is the interferometer. In this arrangement, two or more distant antennas are connected in a way that greatly improves the radio telescope's resolution. (Resolution is the ability to distinguish closely spaced objects.) This and other techniques of improving resolution will be dealt with in a later chapter.

Another difference between optical astronomy and radio astronomy is that the optical telescope is usually operated at a high elevation to minimize the effects of atmospheric distortion. On the other hand, radio telescopes are ideally located in valleys so that their receiving antennas can be shielded as much as possible from terrestrial electrical interference.

Summing up, we can say that optical and radio astronomy are excellent bedfellows, each augmenting the other's usefulness in the field of astronomy.

2 Radio Wave Propagation and the Ionosphere

In the previous chapter we discussed the entire electromagnetic spectrum. Now we are going to narrow our sights to the specific frequencies involved in radio astronomy. We are going to examine the characteristics of radio wave propagation and the effects of the ionosphere, which plays such an important part in radio astronomy.

Let us start by examining the basic nature of a radio wave. When a stone is dropped into a pool of water, the impact of the stone causes ripples, or waves, to radiate equally in all directions away from the point of impact. These ripples have crests and valleys. A radio wave has the same basic characteristics as these water waves, in that it also radiates uniformly in all directions from the point of origin and also consists of crests and valleys.

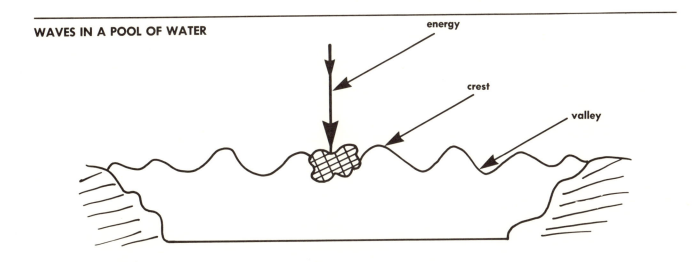

WAVES IN A POOL OF WATER

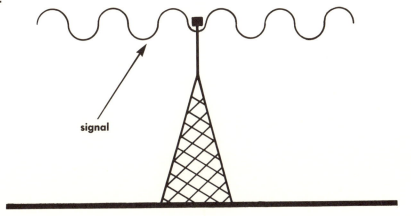

EMITTED RADIO WAVE

PROPERTIES OF RADIO WAVES

One of the fundamental characteristics of radio waves is that their intensity, or energy level, varies inversely with the square of the distance from the point of transmission. That is, the farther away from the point of origin, the weaker these waves become. Their energy is spread over a wider front.

Another basic point is that all radio waves contain two components, the *electrostatic field* and the *electromagnetic field*. These two fields are always at right angles to each other.

Third, radio waves travel at approximately 300 million meters per second.

Wave Polarization

If the lines of force of the emitted wave are parallel to the surface of the earth, the wave is said to be *horizontally polarized*. On the other hand, if the wave is radiated in a vertical plane, then the wave is said to be *vertically polarized*. A third type of polarization, *circular*, is also possible.

THE IONOSPHERE

High above the earth there is an enveloping layer of particles consisting mainly of ions and free electrons and known as the *ionosphere*. This is not just a single layer; rather it consists of several individual layers. Ionization of an atom occurs when it is exposed to an external source of radiation. When this ionization occurs, negatively charged free electrons and postively charged atomic fragments, or ions, are produced. In the case of the ionosphere, the ionizing radiation comes from the sun and other cosmic radiation.

The lowest of these layers is called the *D-layer* and is present only during daylight hours. This layer is caused by the ionization of atmospheric molecules by the strong ultraviolet radiation of sunlight.

Above the D-layer lies the *E-layer*, which also consists of charged electrical particles produced by the sun's ultraviolet radiation. Sometimes the E-layer is divided into two separate regions, the E_1 and E_2 layers.

Going still higher, we come to the *F-layer*. During daylight hours, the F-layer splits into two separate regions, the F_1 and F_2, having approximate heights of 140 and 200 miles above the earth's surface, respectively. Ionospheric layers can block, absorb, or reflect radio energy, depending on the frequency of the signals.

SUNSPOTS AND SOLAR STORMS

In addition to the sun's normal output of ultraviolet radiation, *sunspots*, *solar storms*, and *solar flares* also have an effect on the ionosphere.

Solar storms are electromagnetic disturbances

THE IONOSPHERE

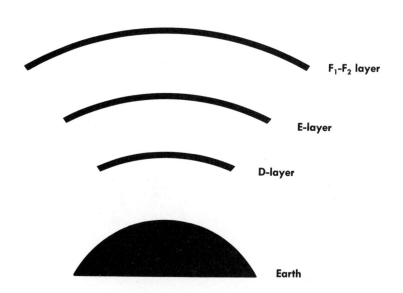

that cover large areas of the sun's surface. These solar storms eject great quantities of charged particles, some of which travel through space until they hit the earth's ionosphere.

These charged particles travel much more slowly than the speed of light because of their mass, and they may take several days to reach the earth's ionosphere. The effect of these particles on the ionosphere is to cause greater ionization. In turn, this causes greater absorption of radio signals passing through the ionosphere. In cases of extremely intense radiation from the sun, a visible aurora can be seen in the northern latitudes. The energy emitted from solar flares is many times that of solar storms. In extreme cases, these solar flares have been intense enough to disrupt electrical power here on earth. It is interesting to note that, while solar storms may last for days or even weeks, solar flares may last for only a few hours.

Sunspots are localized disturbances on the sun's surface which increase and decrease in a cyclic fashion. It has been determined that these disturbances peak about every 11 years.

The two regions of major interest as far as extraterrestrial signals are concerned are the E-layer and the F-layer. Two major features of these layers are their height and their critical frequency. Their height indicates the region of maximum ionization, and their critical frequency, sometimes referred to as *MUF* (minimum usable frequency), is the lowest frequency of radio wave that can pass through them to the earth's surface. The MUF will vary from about 16 to 20 MHz. Variations are generally caused by the sunspot cycle, and general solar radiation will do the same.

During daylight hours the F-layer divides into the F_1 and F_2 layers. The upper F_2 layer varies in height from 250 to 400 miles, while the F_1 layer lies about 150 miles above the earth's surface.

The top layer, F_2, is the one more affected by solar radiation, as it is the layer nearer to the sun. At night, these two layers merge to form a single layer. In passing through these layers, radio energy below the critical wavelength is absorbed or attenuated by the ionized particles.

EXTRATERRESTRIAL SIGNAL ATTENUATION

The ionosphere consists of several layers of charged particles—positive ions and free electrons—which absorb radio frequency energy passing through them.

TROPOSPHERIC REFRACTION OF RADIO SIGNALS

When you place a pencil into a glass of water, you notice that the pencil appears to be bent at the point where it enters the water. This is an example of refraction, or the bending of wave energy. By the same token, incoming extraterrrestrial radio waves are refracted by the earth's troposphere, where a temperature discontinuity exists between it and higher layers of air. The amount of refraction will depend to some extent on the troposphere's temperature and barometric pressure.

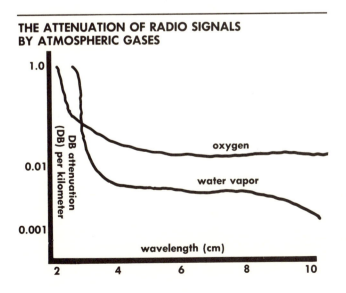

THE DOPPLER EFFECT

If you have ever stood by a railroad track, you may have noticed that the sound of an approaching train's whistle appears to increase in pitch as the train approaches and then decrease as the train goes by. This is known as the *Doppler effect* and occurs at all frequencies.

This Doppler effect is a result of the sound waves compressing, or becoming shorter in wavelength, as their source approaches the observer. As the waves pass by the observer, the waves will stretch out, becoming longer in wavelength.

This Doppler effect is very important in astronomy, as it explains the *red shift* of extraterrestrial objects.

METEOR SHOWERS

When a meteor breaks up as it enters our atmosphere, it becomes superheated as a result of atmospheric friction. When this occurs, these meteor fragments become ionized and then are electrically conductive. As such, they are capable of reflecting terrestrial and extraterrestrial radio signals.

3 Extraterrestrial Radio Sources

It is interesting to note that not all extraterrestrial objects emit radio signals. Also, many cosmic objects are very strong radio signal emitters but emit very little optical radiation.

The *radio window* is that range of frequencies from about 18 MHz to over 30 GHz. The low end of the window is limited by signal absorption in the ionosphere, while the upper limit is determined by signal attenuation caused by water vapor and carbon dioxide suspended in the atmosphere.

THERMAL AND NONTHERMAL RADIATION

What causes the stars and galaxies to produce radio signals? There are two basic causes: thermal and nonthermal radiation.

Thermal radiation is produced either by hot stars, such as our sun, or by clouds of hot, ionized hydrogen gas. Any object heated above absolute zero will emit electromagnetic radiation. As the temperature increases, the frequency of the energy radiated from the object will increase. If an object is hot enough, it becomes incandescent. Its radiation is then in the visible portion of the electromagnetic spectrum. With still further heating, the radiation from the object will shift to the ultraviolet range, and so on.

The accompanying graph shows the intensity of emitted radiation versus frequency for a thermal stellar radio source. The maximum radiation occurs at the visible end of the electromagnetic spectrum, decreasing as the frequency drops toward the radio frequency end of the spectrum. Although the radio energy emitted by the source is much less than that in the visible region, sensitive radio telescopes can detect signals in these microwave regions.

The second form of thermal radiation is from the emission of ionized hydrogen. This radiation is the result of electrons being temporarily detached from the parent hydrogen atoms. These detached electrons are raised to a higher energy level by a source of external energy. When these electrons drop back down to their original energy level, they release their stored energy in the form of radiation. A cloud of hydrogen gas heating up from gravitational collapse, or close to a nearby star, will be ionized in this way and emit radio energy.

THERMAL AND NONTHERMAL RADIO EMISSION

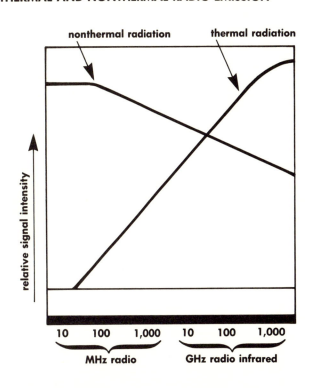

NONTHERMAL SYNCHROTRON RADIATION

Although the mechanism of nonthermal radiation is not completely understood, it is believed to be the result of the so-called *synchrotron process.* This phenomenon occurs when highly charged particles, generally electrons, pass through a magnetic field. With a sufficiently intense magnetic field, and electron velocities approaching the speed of light, intense radio signals will be generated. The effect is similar to the radiation produced by synchrotron devices, where high-energy particles are made to interact with intense man-made magnetic fields.

A unique form of radio signal emission is produced by Jupiter and its moon Io. This very intense signal, measured in millions of watts, occurs in the range of 20–24 MHz. This radiation is a result of the intense magnetic fields surrounding Jupiter interacting with the liquid sodium surface of Io. The effect is the same as passing a conductor through a magnetic field, as in the case of an electric generator. In the case of Jupiter and Io, the conductor is the seething sodium on the surface of the moon. Later, you will learn how to build a radio telescope to receive these Jovian signals.

EXTENDED AND DISCRETE RADIO SOURCES

Throughout this book, you will see references made to extended and discrete radio sources. An *extended signal* appears as a smooth increase and decrease in received signal versus time on a strip chart recording. This type of curve indicates that many extraterrestrial signals are being received at the same time. A good example of an extended source is the Milky Way, which contains many individual radio sources.

A *discrete* radio signal is one radiated from a single point, such as a single star or a small group of stars viewed from Earth. Our sun appears as a discrete radio source.

An optical analogy to the extended source would be viewing a large city at nighttime at a great height. All the city lights would tend to blend together into an apparently single source of light. On the other hand, a single searchlight viewed at the same great distance would be analogous to a discrete source.

If we could view our own galaxy at a great distance with a radio telescope, we would see that the Milky Way is surrounded by a more or less uniform band of radio signal radiation.

When viewed with a radio telescope, the Milky Way appears as a very intense extended radio source, with the point of maximum signal radiation occurring at its center. The reason for this very large signal output is the many radio-emitting sources in the Milky Way. The range of frequencies coming

THE RADIO HALO

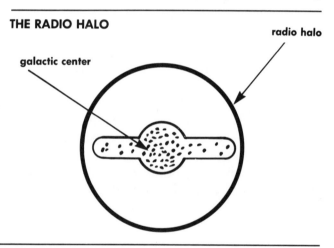

EXTENDED AND DISCRETE RADIO SOURCES

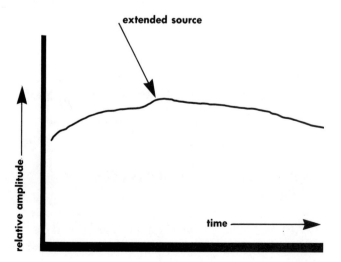
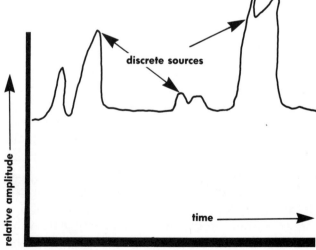

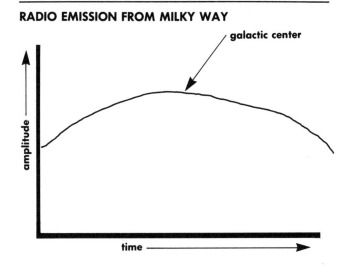

from the various radio sources in the Milky Way is from 20 MHz all the way up to 30 GHz. Because of the intensity of these signals, the amateur radio astronomer can receive them with the simplest of equipment.

GALACTIC AND EXTRAGALACTIC RADIO SOURCES

There are two broad categories of extraterrestrial radio sources: galactic sources, which are present in our own galaxy, and extragalactic sources, which lie outside our galaxy.

Our galaxy contains a large number of radio sources, many of which are remnants of supernova explosions. A typical example of this is the Crab nebula, which was first observed by the Chinese in A.D. 1054.

Traveling farther out into the cosmos, we find a number of distant galaxies that are strong sources of radio energy. One of these sources is Cygnus A, which emits a very intense radio signal. It is interesting to note that, while Cygnus A is a very strong radio emitter, it is very hard to see, because of its great distance from Earth. But Cygnus A's radio signal is so intense that it can be received by the simplest of amateur radio telescopes. There are many thousands of such sources scattered throughout the universe.

THE HYDROGEN LINE

One of the sources of thermal radiation is ionized hydrogen. "Cold," or neutral, hydrogen atoms also emit radio waves but by a different method. The atoms of all elements can absorb or emit energy at specific frequencies. Each type of atom has its own specific frequency; no two of these specific frequencies are the same. Depending on the element, this absorption, or emitting, frequency can range anywhere from microwave to X-ray radiation. Thus it is possible to determine the particular element by observing its so-called spectral lines, or spectral emission.

The neutral hydrogen atom has a frequency of 1,340 MHz (1.34 GHz). By tuning a radio telescope to this frequency, it is possible to detect neutral hydrogen radio sources.

In addition to hydrogen molecules, many organic molecules have been located by means of radio astronomy. These organic molecules include ammonia, methane, benzene, and ethyl alcohol. One scientist figured that there are enough ethyl alcohol molecules in our galaxy to make a martini with a volume equal to that of the earth.

Of particular interest is the discovery of formic acid and methenamine. When these two molecules combine, they form glycine, the simplest of all amino acids. The next step would be the formation of simple protein, the building block of all living matter as we know it. As shown in the accompanying table, many additional molecules have been detected.

OUR SUN

Being the closest radiant energy source to Earth, the sun provides the strongest extraterrestrial radio signal. During World War II, British army radar units experienced interference in their radar receivers, which operated in the 4–6-meter range. The British thought that the Germans had developed a new jamming method, but it was later determined that the Germans' "secret weapon" was actually high-intensity solar-flare radio emission occurring at the same frequency as the British radar.

The radio signal output from the sun is determined by three basic states: the quiet sun, the slowly varying component, and the excited state.

Radio-wave emission from the quiet sun extends from the centimeter range to wavelengths of less than a meter. The frequency of the radiation is determined by the area of the sun from which the signals are originating. For example, waves in the centimeter range originate from the sun's photosphere, while the longer wavelengths are developed in the area of the sun's corona.

Further, in the frequency range of 1 cm to about 10 cm, the size of the radio solar disc appears only slightly larger than the optical solar disc. At the lower frequencies, however, the apparent solar disc is considerably larger. The reason for this is that we are receiving signals from the corona, which extends outward from the sun.

The slowly varying component is caused by sunspots, which will cause the overall level of radio radiation from the sun to increase. This signal increase, or enhancement, may last for days or weeks. Often the increase will vary in step with the sun's 27-day rotation. The pattern of the radio signal radiating above the sunspots has been determined to be essentially the same size as the underlying spot. Additionally, the signal is circularly polarized rather than randomly polarized. Since these signals are circularly polarized, it is believed they are produced by electrons gyrating in the sunspot's localized intense magnetic field.

The intensity of the radiation from the excited sun is many magnitudes greater than that from the quiet sun. A typical solar flare outburst may release more energy than the detonation of 2,400 million megatons of TNT.

The rapidly varying solar activity of an excited sun can be classified as follows: (1) noise storms (Type I), (2) slow drift bursts (Type II), (3) fast drift bursts (Type III), (4) Broad-band emission (Type IV), and (5) continuous emission at meter wavelengths (Type V).

Immediately after the appearance of a visible flare, short bursts of radio energy are emitted from the flare. The frequencies of these bursts will range from about 500 MHz slowly moving downward to about 80 MHz. These are the fast-moving Type III bursts, which are believed to be the result of plasma oscillations generated by the release of high-energy electrons interacting with the sun's intense magnetic field. At times, this Type III burst is accompanied by the broad-band, low-frequency Type V bursts.

A solar flare will first appear optically as a small area of infrared brightness on the sun's surface. The enhancement occurs suddenly, then decays rather slowly. Sometimes, large archlike flares extend up through the sun's atmosphere. This optical solar-flare emission is generally accompanied by very intense ultraviolet, X-ray, and gamma radiation, which reaches the earth about 8 minutes later, causing intense ionizaton of the ionosphere. This effect is called *sudden ionospheric disturbance* (SID) and will often disrupt shortwave radio communication.

During large flares, a stream of high-energy cosmic-ray particles is emitted and reaches the earth

SOLAR RADIO EMISSION

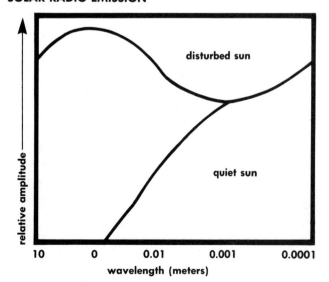

COMPARISON OF OPTICAL AND RADIO SOLAR FLARES

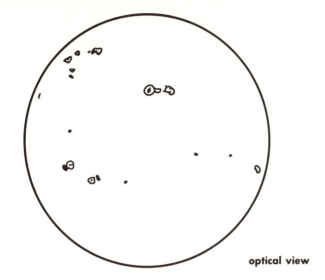
optical view

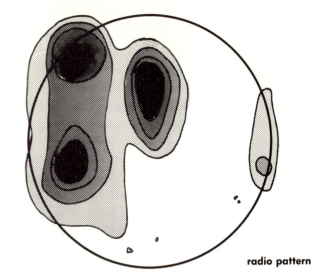
radio pattern

about 24 to 48 hours after the first occurrence of the flare. This stream travels at a speed of approximately 2,000 miles per hour. When this stream of charged particles reaches the earth's Van Allen belt (the magnetic field surrounding the earth), magnetic storms and the aurora result.

THE PLANETS

Until fairly recently, it was assumed that the planets in our solar system, with the exception of Jupiter, did not emit any radio-frequency energy. However, scientists working at the radio astronomy branch of the U.S. Naval Research Laboratories found this to be untrue. Scientists were able to detect very faint signals from the planets. In the centimeter frequency range the radiation from the planets is thermal in nature and is weak. Special receiving techniques were required to detect the minuscule incoming signals. The heart of the receiving system was a maser amplifier, which provided the required low-noise receiver. The receivers were operated in the centimeter frequency range in order to obtain the greatest signal output.

RADIATION FROM JUPITER

Jupiter is unique among the planets in that it emits a very intense radio signal, involving millions of watts of energy.

One of the major differences between Jupiter's radio emission and that of the other cosmic radio sources is that Jupiter's frequency output is between 20 and 24 MHz. This is in contrast to other extraterrestrial radio sources, whose radio frequency is no lower than about 80 MHz.

METEORS

If you stand outside on a clear night, chances are you will see one or more "shooting stars," or meteors. The naked eye can observe about 2 to 10 meteors per hour, depending on the season and time of night. At certain times during the year, the number of observed meteors will increase sharply, reaching as many as 100 or more per hour. These are called meteor showers, and they appear to originate from a specific point in the sky, which is called the *radiant* of the shower.

The casual observer can detect only a few of the total number of meteors descending toward Earth for several reasons. First, the eye's vision covers only a small portion of the total sky. Second, we see only the brighter meteors; there are many more whose brightness is too low to be observed.

The meteor is of interest to the radio astronomer because meteors leave trails of ionized electrons and other ionized particles on their path to the earth's surface. These *meteor trails* have the property of reflecting radio signals, much as does the ionosphere.

There are several nonoptical methods of detecting meteors and meteor showers. The first method is the radio echo technique. The basis of this procedure is to transmit a series of radio frequency pulses skyward. The chosen frequency is well above the cutoff frequency of the ionosphere (18–20 MHz). Transmission frequencies are generally between 80 and 150 MHz.

When the radio pulse encounters meteors or a meteor shower, an echo is returned to the receiver. A counter is attached to the receiver to determine the number of meteors per hour.

The second detection method employs a standard broadcast station whose transmitting antenna is located over the earth's horizon from the receiving location. The best choice is a commercial FM station, as it will transmit a constant carrier level (only the frequency varies). In the absence of a meteor shower, the VHF signal will travel straight and will not bend over the horizon, as low-frequency signals will. The ionized meteor trails will act as an "artificial ionosphere," bending the transmitted FM signal around the curvature of the earth to the receiver. A meteor receiver using this technique will be described later in this book.

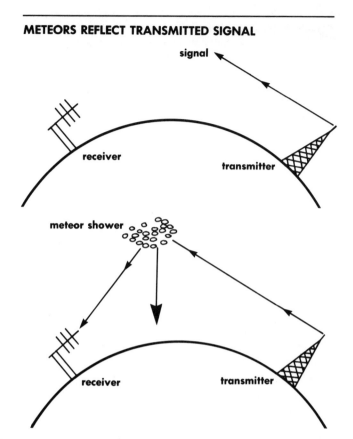

METEORS REFLECT TRANSMITTED SIGNAL

4 Some Optical Astronomy Basics

A general understanding of the basics of optical astronomy will greatly aid the amateur radio astronomer, because he will be able to locate the sources of many radio signals with a conventional telescope.

REFRACTOR TELESCOPE

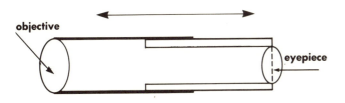

REFRACTOR TELESCOPE (*Courtesy Edmund Scientific Co.*)

OPTICAL TELESCOPES

There are four basic optical telescope configurations: refractors, reflectors, Schmidt-Cassegrain types, and rich field telescopes.

The first optical telescope was invented by Galileo in 1608. Galileo's telescope was of the refractor type. In this arrangement, the incoming light waves are gathered by the objective lens and focused on the eyepiece. Focusing is accomplished by sliding the inner tube in or out to obtain the clearest image. A photo of a typical refractor telescope is shown.

In 1672, Sir Isaac Newton invented the reflector telescope. The Newtonian reflector differs from the refractor in that it employs a mirror as the primary focusing device rather than a lens. A typical Newtonian telescope is shown in the accompanying photo.

The Schmidt-Cassegrain telescope employs both a primary mirror and a secondary mirror. The Schmidt telescope differs from the Newtonian telescope in several respects. In the Schmidt telescope, a secondary mirror is employed to "fold back" the incoming rays. Because of this arrangement of ray travel, the telescope can be made shorter, and this has its mechanical advantages. One disadvantage of the Schmidt telescope for the amateur is that its optics are a bit more complicated and their alignment is more critical.

The rich field telescope is a relatively new development, and although generally lower in magnification than the Newtonian and Schmidt types, the rich field has a number of advantages. First, because of its small size and light weight, its mounting requirements are simplified. Second, the rich field telescope provides an erect image, so it can be used to view terrestrial objects. Third, the rich field telescope provides a much wider viewing angle than the Newtonian and Schmidt telescopes.

REFLECTING TELESCOPE *(Courtesy Meade Instruments)*

SCHMIDT-CASSEGRAIN TELESCOPES *(Courtesy Meade Instruments)*

SCHMIDT-CASSEGRAIN

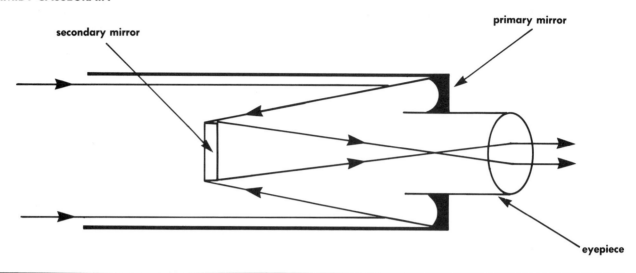

RICH FIELD TELESCOPE *(Courtesy Edmund Scientific Co.)*

Some Optical Astronomy Basics

Light-Gathering Ability and Magnification

The newcomer to optical astronomy generally assumes that the higher the telescope's magnification, the better the unit. While good image magnification is of course desirable, equally important is the telescope's light-gathering ability. This is determined primarily by the size of the telescope's primary optical system—a glass lens in the case of the refractor or a mirror in the case of the reflecting telescope. The telescope's image magnification is provided by the eyepiece.

An overall requirement of any telescope, optical or radio, is good resolution. What we mean by *resolution* is the ability of a telescope, at a particular magnification, to sharply separate objects that lie very close together in the viewing field. Two point sources viewed through a telescope with poor resolution tend to blur together. Good resolution means that you can see more detail. In general, for optical telescopes, resolution decreases with increasing magnification and in fact limits the useful magnification of a particular instrument. The degree of resolution, all other things being equal, depends on the diameter of the telescope's primary lens or mirror. The larger the primary mirror, the greater the resolution.

This same concept holds true with a radio telescope. The primary lens, or mirror, of the optical telescope finds its equivalent in the antenna of the radio telescope. The larger the antenna, the greater the radio telescope's resolution. Furthermore, the optical telescope's magnification is equivalent to the electronic amplification of the radio telescope.

STAR POSITIONS

If you stand outside on a clear night and face south, you will notice that the stars and planets appear to move from east to west across the heavens. This apparent motion of the celestial bodies is due of course to the rotation of the earth.

To measure a celestial object's position, it is convenient to envision a large sphere with the earth at its center. The two basic coordinates that determine the celestial object's position are *declination*, which is the same as latitude on earth, and *right ascension*, which corresponds to longitude on earth. The celestial poles are the points on the celestial sphere directly above the earth's geographic poles. The ce-

POOR VERSUS GOOD TELESCOPE RESOLUTION

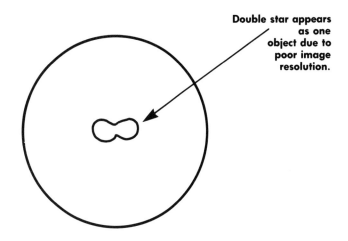

Double star appears as one object due to poor image resolution.

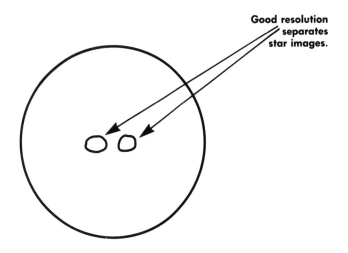

Good resolution separates star images.

lestial equator is a line drawn halfway between the North and South poles. Declination is measured in degrees, minutes, and seconds of arc, north or south of the celestial equator. Right ascension is measured from 0 to 24 hours of time from west to east.

Every year at March 21 (the vernal equinox), the sun intersects the first point of Aries, and this is the point from which right ascension is determined. This is similar to determining the earth's longitude from a specific line, such as the Greenwich prime meridian. The exact position of a star or constellation can easily be determined, much as a specific point on earth can be located using latitude and longitude.

THE CELESTIAL SPHERE

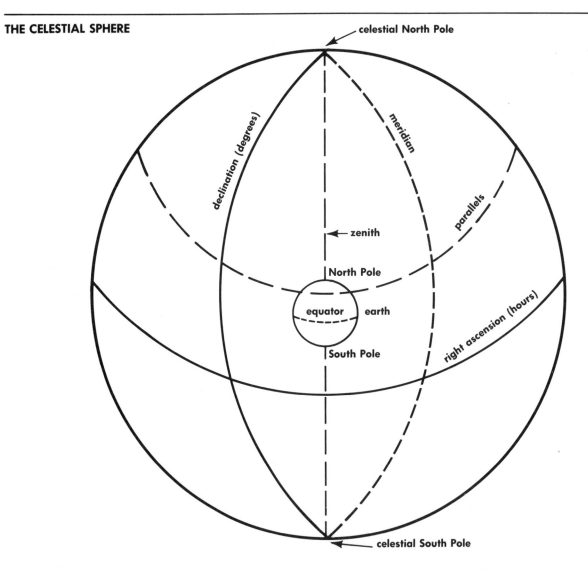

SIGNAL PROCESSING

Whether an optical or radio telescope is used, suitable means must be provided for interpreting and presenting the received signal. In the case of the optical telescope, the method is simply viewing the desired object through the telescope's eyepiece. Adding a bit of sophistication, we can attach a camera to the telescope's eyepiece in order to obtain a permanent record of the object. A more advanced method now being employed with optical telescopes is the use of photon counters. These remarkably sensitive detectors are glorified "electric eyes," or photoelectric cells, and are sensitive enough to detect individual photons. As a result, these detectors are many times more sensitive than the fastest photographic emulsion.

In the case of radio astronomy, the simplest signal-processing method is the strip chart recorder, which provides a graph of the received signal. While this is satisfactory for relatively simple observations and is generally appropriate for the amateur radio astronomer, use of a computer enables the generation of actual "pictures" of the radio signals.

APERTURE SYNTHESIS AND VARIABLE RESOLUTION

A typical example of a modern, completely computerized radio telescope is the VLA (Very Large Array) installation located at Socorro, New Mexico. This system consists of a Y-shaped array of individual parabolic antennas. The VLA is used to produce radio pictures with as much detail as those made by an optical telescope. To accomplish this with a single antenna at radio wavelengths would require building an antenna about 27 kilometers in diameter. Instead, we can place many smaller antennas in a Y pattern with each arm of the Y 21 kilometers long. By combining the data from all the antennas and using the rotation of the earth, we can synthesize a radio picture equivalent to one produced by a monstrous 27-kilometer single antenna.

The resolution of the array can be varied by changing the distance separating the antennas. Different astronomical observations require different resolutions. A high-resolution image would be needed to probe the inner core of a galaxy, but only a low-resolution image could reveal the large, faint overall structure of that galaxy. The antennas of the VLA can be moved in and out on each arm, achieving an effect somewhat similar to a zoom lens on a camera.

The array is generally found in one of four standard configurations, ranging from one where the antennas are all crowded to within 0.6 kilometers (2,000 feet) of the array's center, to one where the antennas stretch out to 21 kilometers (13 miles) from the center. This largest array gives the finest detail in a radio image.

In the control building, the cosmic radio signals from each antenna are extracted from the waveguide, amplified again, then converted into numbers that represent the signal strength. Then, in a special purpose computer, the signal from each antenna is multiplied with the signal from every other antenna. This multiplication is repeated 100 million times a second.

PROCESSING THE SIGNALS

Without computers, operation of the VLA would be impossible. The control of the array is by computer. Computers are also continually monitoring the performance of thousands of components in the antennas and in the control building. In some cases, replacement parts are automatically switched in when an error is detected. In the control room the array operator monitors these computer systems and can respond if a problem occurs.

The radio images themselves are stored as numbers in a computer, which can display them as colors or as shades of gray. The most intensive use of computers at the VLA involves calculations to form and analyze these images. Rushing along at tens of millions of operations a second, the computers can just keep up with the flow of data from the array.

The data taken with the VLA are stored on magnetic tape. An astronomer can therefore recreate a radio image days or even years after the actual observations are made. A single radio image may require 40 hours of observations for great detail, or it may require only five minutes of data for a crude "snapshot."

5 Some Basic Electronics

We are going to examine some basic electronic and electrical devices as applicable to radio astronomy. Although not intended as a complete course in electronics, the material covered will be of benefit to the amateur astronomer who is knowledgeable about optical astronomy but weak in radio theory.

ELECTRONIC SYMBOLS AND CIRCUITS

As in the case of mechanical blueprints, which have special symbols and designations, electronic wiring diagrams, or schematics, as they are called, also have their own particular symbols. Some familiarity with these symbols and basic electronic circuitry is necessary to develop a working knowledge of how radio telescopes receive and process signals. The accompanying table lists the most commonly used electronic symbols.

VOLTAGE, CURRENT, AND RESISTANCE

The three basic quantities of an electrical circuit are voltage, current, and resistance. *Voltage*, or electromotive force (EMF), is the unit of electrical "pressure" and is measured in *volts*. The greater the voltage, the greater the electrical "pressure." A flashlight battery has a voltage of about 1.5 volts and can energize a small light bulb against its internal resistance. A power line with 120 volts produces a much higher electrical "pressure" and can drive household appliances containing electric motors of various kinds. While voltage is a measure of electrical "pressure," *current* is a measure of the *amount* of electrical flow. The greater the electric current, the more electrons set in motion. The unit of current is the *ampere*. *Resistance* is a measure of the retarding force in an electrical circuit. The unit of resistance is the *ohm*.

OHM'S LAW

There is a definite relationship between voltage, current, and resistance. Ohm's Law is expressed as follows: $E = I \times R$

where E = voltage
I = current
R = resistance

As an example of how Ohm's Law is applied in an electrical circuit, let's assume we have a power source of 12 volts and a resistance of 2 ohms in the circuit. What is the value of the current flow in the circuit? Transposing Ohm's Law:

$$I = \frac{E}{R} = \frac{12}{2} = 6 \text{ amps}$$

POWER

Power is a measure of the amount of work performed in a specific period of time and is the product of voltage and current, expressed as follows:

$$\text{Power (in watts)} = E \times I$$
$$\text{or} \quad I^2 \times R$$
$$\text{or} \quad \frac{E^2}{R}$$

As an example of how the power formula is used, we can determine the wattage of an incandescent light bulb if the applied voltage is 100 volts and the current is one ampere.

$$P = E \times I$$
$$P = 100 \times I = 100 \text{ watts}$$

ELECTRONIC SYMBOLS *(Courtesy Radio Relay League)*

RESISTANCE AND RESISTORS

In almost all electronic circuits, you will find resistance used. The main purpose of this resistance is to limit the flow of current in a particular circuit. Incidentally, all electrical conductors have a certain amount of inherent electrical resistance at temperatures above absolute zero. However, this resistance is generally low enough to be of no concern.

The two major properties of a resistor are its resistance, which is measured in ohms, and its power-dissipation rating, which is expressed in watts.

There are several different resistor types, including carbon resistors and wire-wound resistors. The carbon, or *composition*, resistors are generally rated at from 0.25 to 2 watts in power dissipation. The larger, wire-wound resistors come in sizes from 5 watts up to 1,000 watts or more.

Resistors are available in a wide range of resistance values, going from under 1 ohm to 20 meg (20,000,000) ohms. The larger, wire-wound resistors generally are not available in ranges much higher than about 100,000 ohms.

Another rating given to resistors is the *tolerance*, or permissible variation, in the specified value of resistance, expressed as a percentage. In the case of standard composition resistors, tolerances are generally 20%, 10%, and 5%. Special precision resistors are available with tolerances as low as 0.5%. In most electronic circuits a resistance change of ± 10% of the nominal value is satisfactory. Most composition resistors have their resistance value indi-

Some Basic Electronics

VARIOUS RESISTOR TYPES

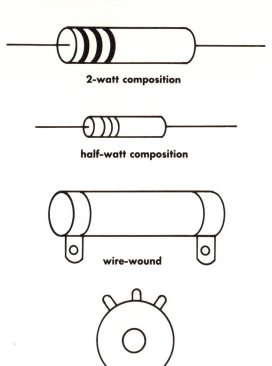

cated by colored bands around their bodies.

Potentiometers are variable resistors. The volume control on your TV or stereo is a potentiometer. Potentiometers are fitted with a shaft or variable connection of some sort, which is turned to vary their resistance.

CAPACITORS

The *capacitor* is another essential component of electronic circuits. While it is possible to go into a lot of math describing the operation of capacitors, two basic statements about them will be satisfactory for our purposes: Capacitors are similar to batteries in that they can store an applied electric voltage or charge and capacitors will pass alternating current (AC) but will block direct current (DC).

There are two basic categories of capacitor, fixed and variable. In turn, these can be divided into specific types: mica, paper, ceramic, polyester film, and electrolytic. These designations refer to the dielectric material used in the capacitor.

The unit of capacitance is the *farad*. The farad is much too large a unit for practical use in most circuits, so we commonly employ microfarads or picofarads. The *microfarad* is one millionth of a farad, while the *picofarad* is one millionth of a microfarad. A typical electrolytic capacitor would have a value of 100 microfarads, or a small mica capacitor might have a capacitance value of 0.01 microfarad. The amount of electric charge, or voltage, that a capacitor can hold is determined by the value of its capacitance. For example, a 10-microfarad capacitor will hold 10 times the charge of a 1-microfarad capacitor.

To simplify matters, we use abbreviations in denoting capacitance values. A 1-microfarad capacitor would be listed as 1 MF. Often capacitor values much below 0.001 MF are listed in picofarads, so a 0.001-MF capacitor would be a 1,000-pf unit. As you can see, all we do is move the decimal point.

Generally speaking, capacitors with values of 1 MF or less are made of either paper, film, or mica. Capacitors with values much above 1 MF are generally of the electrolytic type.

Electrolytic capacitors are different from the other types in that they are *polarized*. As a result, it

VARIOUS CAPACITOR TYPES

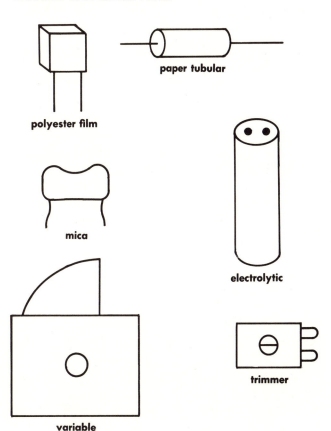

is essential that the proper polarity of these capacitors be observed when connecting them into a circuit. Electrolytic capacitors are most generally used in electronic power supply circuits.

Variable Capacitors

Unlike the capacitors just described, which have a fixed value of capacitance, variable capacitors have means, generally a shaft, to vary their capacitance value. A familiar example of a variable capacitor is the frequency-tuning dial on your radio. While fixed capacitors have solid dielectrics, variable capacitors generally have air dielectrics.

In addition to capacitance values, all capacitors have maximum applied DC voltage ratings, which must not be exceeded. If the rated voltage is exceeded the capacitor will "blow." Typical voltage ratings range from 6 volts to 600 volts, DC. The reason for this DC voltage rating is that all capacitors consist of plate or foil electrodes separated by an insulating material called the *dielectric*. If the voltage is excessive, it will puncture or arc across the dielectric, causing the capacitor to short circuit.

INDUCTANCE

An *inductor* consists of a coil of wires wound over a core, which may consist of either solid metal or air. While we could go into great detail on the operation of inductance, let's simply state that an inductor will tend to oppose an alternating current applied through it, while readily passing direct current. This is just the opposite of a capacitor, which will pass AC and block DC. The unit of inductance is the *henry*. As in the case of farads, the henry is often broken down into smaller values, particularly in radio circuits. Typical values are the *millihenry* (Mhy) and *microhenry* (uhy).

Inductors are also sometimes called *chokes*, particularly when they are used in electronic power filter circuits.

Inductors with solid cores are used in low-frequency applications such as power supply filters. The air-core inductors are employed in radio circuits, where the energy loss of the solid-metal core would be excessive. There are exceptions to this; for example, certain RF inductors employ ferrite materials in their cores.

Adjustable inductors are also available, and these consist of a coil of wire wound over a nonmetallic form, inside of which is an adjustable ferrite "slug," which can be moved in or out of the coil by means of an adjusting screw. These coils are used only in RF circuits because it is not normally possible to obtain large values of inductance with these adjustable coils.

Another type of coil is the *toroid inductor*. This kind of coil is wound on a doughnut-shaped circular core and is used mainly in radio frequency circuits.

BASIC ELECTRICAL CIRCUITS

There are two basic electrical circuits, series and parallel. A representative *series* circuit might contain two light bulbs, a switch, and a battery to power the circuit, all connected sequentially on the same wire. When the switch is closed, the two bulbs will light, and since these two bulbs are in series, only *half* of the battery voltage will appear across each bulb (assuming equal bulb wattages). In a *parallel* circuit, the two bulbs would be connected "in parallel" on separate wires, and as a result the *full* battery voltage will appear across each bulb. A *series-parallel* circuit would use both types of connections. In electronic circuits you will find a number of series, series-parallel, and parallel circuits employed.

DIRECT AND ALTERNATING CURRENT

There are two basic types of electrical current flow, *direct current (DC)* and *alternating current (AC)*. Direct current is the type produced by batteries and rectified power supplies. Almost all types of electronic equipment operate from direct current, and AC current must be converted to DC current to be useful here.

BASIC INDUCTANCE

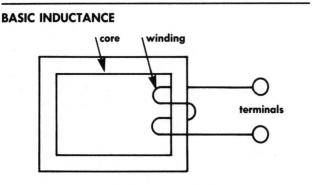

Some Basic Electronics

BASIC SERIES-PARALLEL CIRCUITS

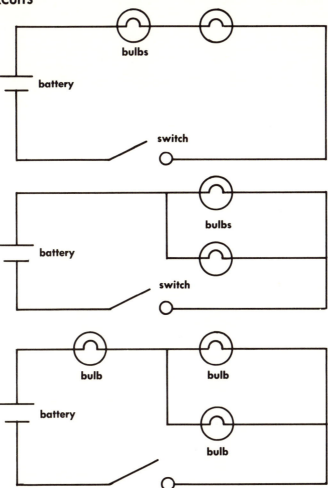

To get an idea of the nature of direct current, imagine a simple circuit featuring a 6-volt battery, a switch, and a resistor connected in series. With the switch in the open position, there will be no current flow and hence no voltage drop across the resistor. Close the switch, and current will flow through the resistor. As long as the switch is closed, current will continue to flow through the circuit *in one direction*.

The important thing to remember about alternating current is that, unlike DC, it is continuously reversing its direction of flow. To clarify this, let us add a polarity-reversing switch to a simple circuit containing a resistor. This circuit is similar to the previous circuit, except that the polarity-reversing switch in effect reverses the battery connections. With the switch in one position, the voltage across the resistor increases in a positive direction. With the switch in the other position, the voltage across the resistor increases in a *negative* direction. From this experiment, we can see that by reversing the battery voltage back and forth we have obtained an *alternating* voltage across the resistor.

Alternating current is the most commonly used type of power, because it is easily produced by large generators and its voltage can be stepped up or down by means of transformers. Large power distribution transformers raise the output from generator powerhouses to 100,000 volts or more for long-distance power transmission. The reason for this high voltage is that a low current can then be moved along smaller diameter, and hence lighter, transmission lines and still transmit the same amount of power. Remember that power is the product of voltage and current. You can raise the voltage and lower the current and still transmit the same amount of *power*.

The high voltage conveyed by these lines is fed to

COMPARISON OF DC AND AC CIRCUITS

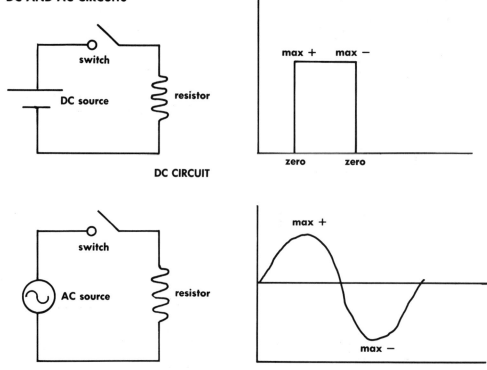

substations where, by means of transformers, it is reduced to about 22,000 volts for further distribution. The voltage is again reduced to 2,200 volts for local businesses and residential customers. Finally, by means of that familiar pole transformer, the 2,200 volts are stepped down to 220 volts for use in your house.

Alternating current is continuously reversing its direction of flow, and the number of times per second the reversal takes place is called the *frequency*. The frequency of an alternating current is expressed in hertz. One cycle per second is equal to one hertz. Standard house current is 60 hertz. It is common practice to abbreviate hertz as Hz.

TRANSFORMERS

The transformer is another important electrical component. The transformer consists of a primary winding, a secondary winding, and a metallic core over which both windings are placed.

If you connect a length of wire to a battery, a magnetic field will be produced around the wire. If we wrap the wire into a coil and pass current through it, the generated magnetic field will increase in direct relation to the number of turns of wire. If the coil is connected to a source of alternating current, with that current continually varying in amplitude, we will get a varying magnetic field generated in the coil.

If we place a second coil or winding next to the coil that has the AC current flowing through it, a current will be induced in the second coil by means of electromagnetic induction. If the two coils are placed on a steel core, the lines of varying magnetic flux will be more effectively coupled between the two coils. This is our basic electrical transformer, a primary winding to which the AC current is applied, and the secondary winding in which the current is induced.

STEP-UP AND STEP-DOWN TRANSFORMERS

One of the useful properties of a transformer is its ability to either step up or step down voltage or current. If, for example, a transformer has 100 primary turns and 10 secondary turns, it would be a *step-down transformer,* as the voltage across the secondary will be less than the primary voltage. The ratio

Some Basic Electronics 33

GENERATION OF MAGNETIC FIELD FROM DC CURRENT

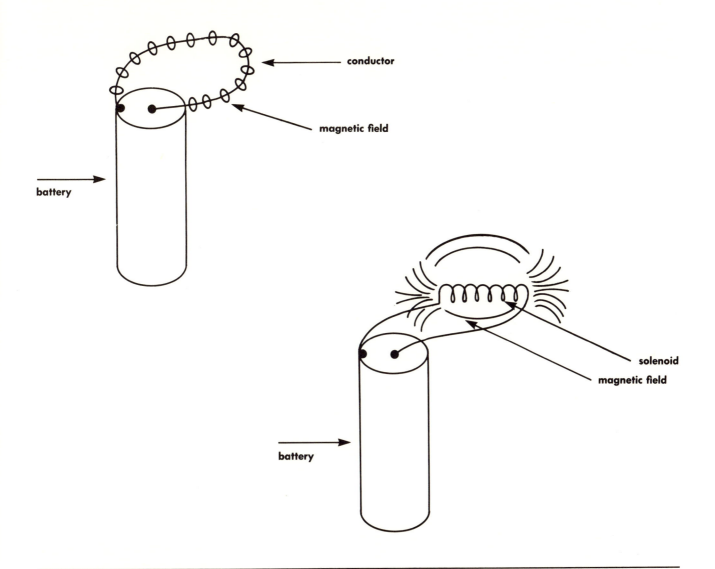

BASIC TRANSFORMER ACTION

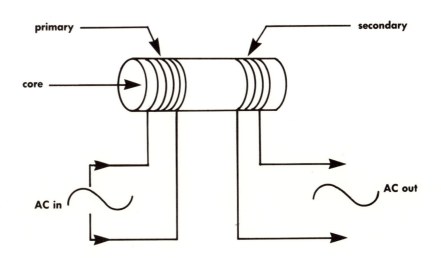

BASIC TRANSFORMER CONFIGURATION

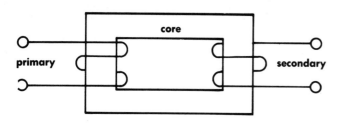

TRANSFORMER SCHEMATIC DIAGRAM

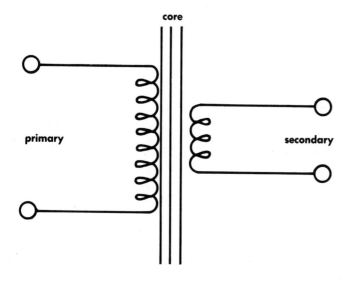

for determining the secondary voltage is as follows:

$$\frac{NP}{NS} = \frac{\text{number of primary turns}}{\text{numbers of secondary turns}}$$

To see how this works out, let's say we have 100 primary turns and 10 secondary turns. This would be

$$\frac{NP}{NS} = \frac{100}{10} = 10$$

So, if we put 100 volts AC into the primary, we will get 10 volts out of the secondary.

On the other hand, if we have more turns on the secondary than on the primary, we will have a *step-up transformer*. The voltage across the secondary will be higher than that applied to the primary.

SEMICONDUCTORS

We are now going to turn our attention to semiconductor devices—diodes, transistors, etc. The *semiconductor diode* is perhaps the simplest of all semiconductor devices. It consists of two types of semiconductor material: the P-type, which contains positive electric charge carriers, and the N-type, which contains negative electric charge carriers. The point where these two materials meet is called the *semiconductor junction*.

Remember that similar electrical charges will repel each other and that dissimiliar electric charges will attract each other. The idea is the same as with a magnet, where two north or two south poles will repel each other, while north and south poles attract each other.

Suppose we construct a circuit with a battery and switch connected to a diode. The positive battery terminal is connected to the P-type material and the negative terminal to the N-type material. The positive charge carrier in the P-type material is repelled by the positive lead from the battery and pushed toward the diode's junction. Similarly, the negative charge in the N-type material is repelled by the battery's negative lead toward the junction.

When the two charges, which are of equal value, reach the junction, they cancel out each other. This effectively *depletes*, or removes, the junction as a barrier between the P-type and N-type materials and current will flow through the diode. In effect, the diode is acting as a closed switch, completing current flow through the circuit.

If the terminals are reversed, with the positive terminal connected to the diode's N-type material and the negative terminal connected to the P-type material, both the positive and negative charges in the diode will be pulled away from the junction. The effect of this is to widen the junction area so that no current can cross it to complete the circuit. This is the same as an open switch. This condition is known as *reverse bias,* and when the diode is conducting, it is *forward biased*.

TRANSISTORS

The transistor is a "sandwich" made of a P-type material, an N-type material, and another P-type material. We now have two junctions rather than just the one in the case of the semiconductor diode.

Some Basic Electronics

The transistor has three leads, one lead to the bottom P-type material, a second lead to the center N-type material, and the third lead to the top P-type material. The bottom lead to the P-type material is called the *emitter*, the center lead is called the *base*, and the top lead is called the *collector*.

Suppose you were to connect a battery, a switch, and a DC current meter between the transistor's emitter and base, and a second battery and meter between the emitter and the collector. When the switch in the emitter-base circuit is closed, the P–N emitter-base junction will become forward biased. When this emitter-base junction is forward biased, current will flow through it, as indicated by the meter. If the positive terminal of the second battery in the base-collector circuit is connected to the collector, there will be a positive electric charge on the collector. The forward-biased emitter-base junction has generated charge carriers in the base region, and they will be attracted into the collector by its positive charge. Remember, unlike electric charges attract.

The forward-biased base-emitter junction generates a large number of negative charge carriers at its junction. The second battery, connected between emitter and collector, places a positive voltage on the collector. This positive voltage generates an electrostatic field, which extends into the collector base region. Since the base-collector junction is so thin (generally less than 0.001 inch), the positive voltage field attracts the negative charge carriers in the base region. As a result, there will be a flow of current between the collector and the emitter.

Transistor Amplifiers

Before getting into an examination of transistor amplifiers, let's take a moment to see just why we need electrical signal amplifiers. Perhaps the most familiar example of an amplifier is the one in your stereo system. In this case, an amplifier is used to boost the very low signal voltage developed by the phono pickup to a level sufficient to drive the speakers. Another example is the amplifier used to boost the minuscule signals arriving at the receiving antenna of a radio telescope. Generally these signals will be less than a millionth of a watt and, as a result, it is necessary to amplify these signals millions of times before they are applied to the final readout device. An amplifier can amplify any desired signal—speech, music, radio telescope signals, etc.—depending on its design.

A typical transistor amplifier circuit consists of an N–P–N transistor, a 2-volt emitter-base bias battery, a collector load resistor, and a 12-volt collector bias battery. The emitter-base junction must be forward biased to permit current to flow through the base-collector junction. This bias is supplied by the emitter-base bias battery. Let's assume that the values of base bias are such as to produce 2 volts at the base of the transistor. This will result in a flow of collector current through the collector load resistor and the collector battery. Since collector current is flowing through the load resistance, there will be a corresponding voltage drop across it. (Remember, when current flows through a resistor, there will be a voltage drop across it; the greater the current, the greater the voltage drop.) Now, let's say that the 2

OPERATION OF SEMICONDUCTOR DIODE

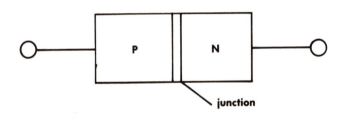

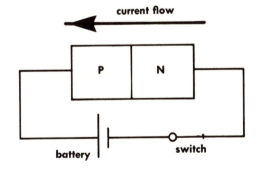

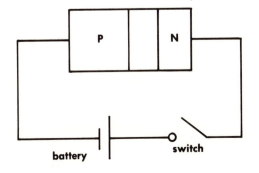

BASIC TRANSISTOR OPERATION

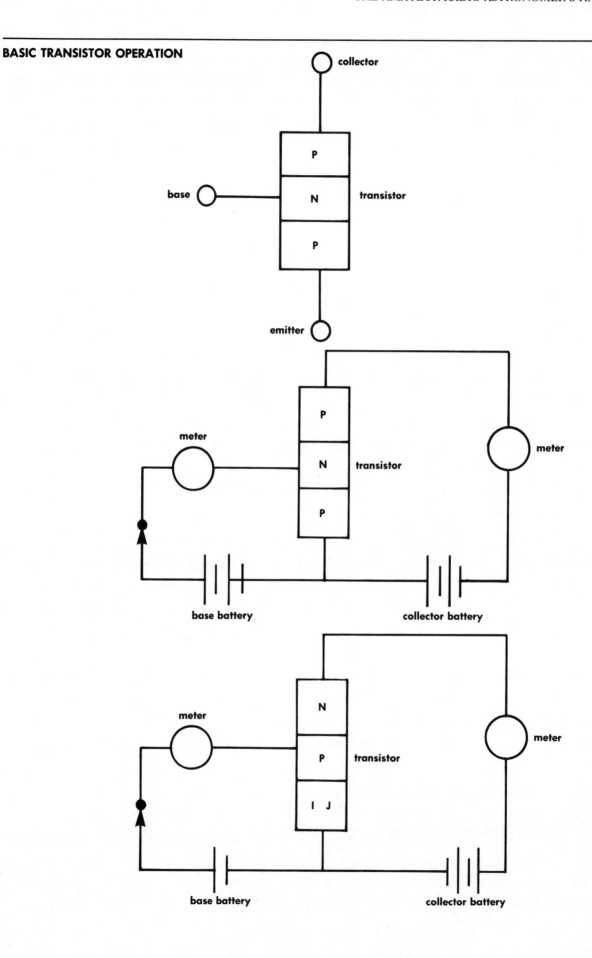

Some Basic Electronics

BASIC AMPLIFIER ARRANGEMENT

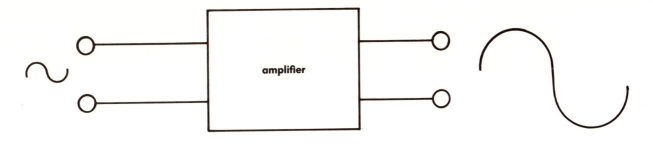

BASIC COMMON-EMITTER TRANSISTOR AMPLIFIER STAGE

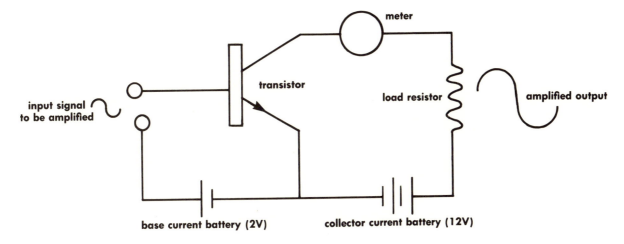

volts on the base of the transistor will produce 6 volts on the collector due to the voltage drop across the load resistance. We now apply the signal to be amplified to the base of the transistor. The amplitude of this input signal voltage is 2 volts peak to peak. Now, let's first consider the positive half-cycle of the input signal. Since it is positive, it will *add* to the existing base bias provided by the battery. In turn, this will cause an increase in transistor collector current. This will result in a larger current flow through the resistor and hence a greater voltage drop across it, and the collector voltage will decrease to +4 volts.

Now, continue with the following negative half-cycle of the input signal. Since this is a negative voltage, it will *subtract* from the existing base bias provided by the base bias battery. This will result in a decrease in emitter-base current and hence a corresponding decrease in collector current. This decreased collector current will mean a corresponding decreased voltage drop across the resistor, and the collector voltage will rise to +8 volts. From this, you can see that we have achieved the desired signal amplification. A 2-volt input signal has been amplified to a 4-volt output signal.

ELECTRONIC POWER SUPPLIES

One of the fundamental components of an electronic device is the direct current power supply. The purpose of the power supply is to convert incoming alternating current to direct current. Almost all semiconductor circuitry must operate from a source of direct current.

Power supplies come in a wide variety of types, sizes, voltages, and current configurations, ranging from less than 6 volts DC at a few milliamperes to 50,000 volts at 1 ampere or more. And, of course, power supplies are used throughout the circuitry of radio telescopes.

The simplest type of power supply is called the half-wave. It consists of a transformer, a P–N junc-

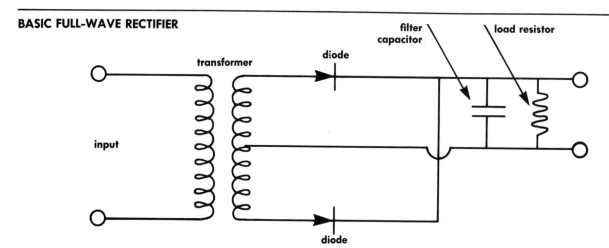

BASIC HALF-WAVE RECTIFIER

BASIC FULL-WAVE RECTIFIER

tion diode, a filter capacitor, and the power supply load. The heart of the circuit is the P–N diode, which performs the actual rectifying action, converting AC to DC. Junction diodes are electric switches, passing current when they are forward biased, blocking current when they are reverse biased.

Let's review the operation of the circuit. First assume that the AC input to the primary coil of the transformer is increasing in the positive direction. By means of transformer action, a voltage will be developed across the transformer's secondary coil, with the "top" of the secondary being positive with respect to the "bottom." This, in turn, will cause the *anode*, the P-type section of the diode, to become positive. Since the diode is now forward biased, current will flow through the circuit. The voltage across the load resistor is half-cycle.

On the following half-cycle of AC input to the transformer, the top of its secondary will now become negative with respect to the bottom. In this case, the diode's P-type material will become negative. As a result, this diode will be reverse biased, and no current will flow through the circuit. From this you can see that the half-wave power supply produces a series of half-cycles of current. This is why it is called a *half-wave rectifier*.

Full-Wave Rectifier

Power supply efficiency can be improved by using a *full-wave rectifier*. Such a circuit consists of a transformer, two P–N diodes, and the power supply load resistor. The power transformer is different from the one used in the half-wave circuit, in that it has a center-tapped secondary winding. This is necessary for full-wave operation.

When the positive half-cycle of the AC input signal is applied to the transformer, the top half of the load resistor becomes positive. The top diode is forward biased. The bottom diode is reverse biased, so no current will flow through it. During the negative-input AC half-cycle, the top of the transformer's secondary now becomes negative and its bottom half becomes positive. As a result, the bottom diode's P-type material becomes positive and will conduct current. Twice as many half-cycles are

Some Basic Electronics

present. Thus the *full-wave* has been rectified.

A *bridge rectifier* employs four rectifier diodes. Like the full-wave rectifier, the bridge rectifier provides a full-wave output. One advantage of the bridge rectifier is that it does not require a center-tapped power transformer.

Power Supply Filters

The output from the rectifier consists of a series of half-cycle pulses. It is the purpose of a power supply to deliver a smooth DC output. As a result, it is necessary to find a means to smooth out the variations from the power supply output. This is accomplished by the power supply filter.

The simplest power supply filter consists of a large-value capacitor connected directly across the power supply output terminals. The resulting waveform shows that the capacitor charges up the power supply output to the peak voltage, then discharges through the power supply load between successive cycles.

While this simple filter illustrates the filtering principle, it is not the best when a load of any magnitude is applied to the power supply. A better arrangement involves two capacitors and an inductor, or *filter choke*.

This material will serve as a good foundation for the electronics associated with amateur radio astronomy.

BASIC BRIDGE RECTIFIER

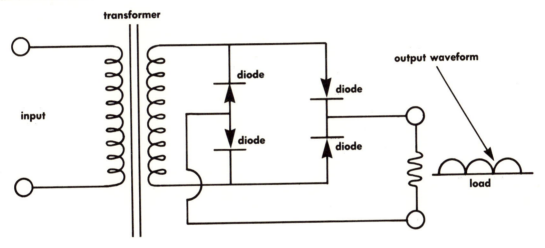

POWER SUPPLY FILTER CIRCUITS

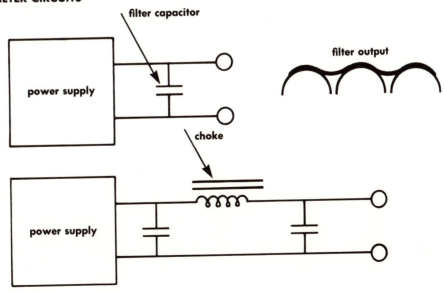

6 Basic Radio Astronomy Systems

We will now examine various types of radio astronomy systems, beginning with the basic configurations and following through with the more advanced systems.

The radio telescope is often called a *radiometer* because it receives electromagnetic radiation from an external source and converts it into electrical energy. Photographic exposure meters are also radiometers, since they convert electromagnetic energy (light) into an electrical signal. In short, any device that converts any wavelength of electromagnetic radiation into a corresponding electrical signal is a radiometer.

The radiometer consists of three basic components: the antenna, the receiver, and a readout device, which may be either a strip chart recorder, a magnetic tape recorder, or a computer.

THE DRIFT RADIOMETER

With a basic drift radiometer, the receiving antenna faces due south. As a result, as the earth "drifts" (rotates), the fixed antenna will be exposed to the "revolving" sky above. Except for special applications, this type of radio telescope stays in a fixed position.

One of the major disadvantages of the simple radiometer is its wide beamwidth. Several discrete radio sources may be in the beam at the same time. As a result it is not possible to distinguish these sources. One solution to the problem is to enlarge the size of the receiving antenna. The larger the antenna, the narrower the received beamwidth. The problem with this is that as antenna size goes up so does cost and mechanical complexity.

THE TWO ANTENNA INTERFEROMETER

A solution to the problem of obtaining a narrow beamwidth without the use of a large receiving antenna is the use of a two antenna *interferometer*. The arrangement consists of two antennas con-

THE RADIOMETER RADIO TELESCOPE

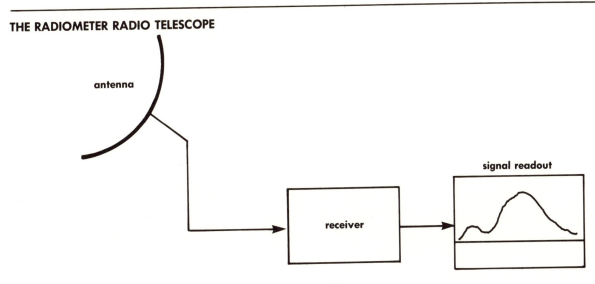

nected in parallel to the input of the radio telescope receiver. The resulting output waveform, as recorded on a strip chart recorder, is fan shaped and composed of a number of individual lobes.

The angular width of each lobe, and therefore the angular revolving pattern, or narrowness of the beamwidth, is determined by both the wavelength and the distance between the two antennas. For example, if we keep the same antenna spacing but increase the receiving frequency, we will decrease the effective antenna beamwidth. Similarly, we can decrease the beamwidth by keeping the same fre-

A SINGLE ANTENNA CAN'T SEPARATE CLOSELY SPACED OBJECTS

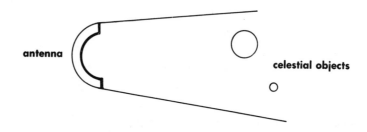

THE INTERFEROMETER RADIO TELESCOPE

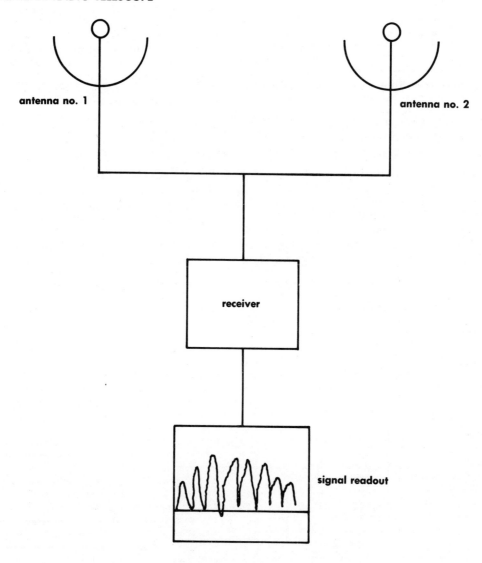

Basic Radio Astronomy Systems

quency but increasing the antenna spacing. This is expressed by the formula:

$$\Delta \delta = \frac{\lambda}{d}$$

where: $\Delta \delta$ = angle between successive minimum and maximum points of the lobes
λ = wavelength of receiving system
d = distance (baseline) between antennas

As can be seen from the above equation, the effective beamwidth can be reduced by increasing the frequency or the baseline, or both.

Because of its more effective signal resolution, the interferometer can offer information as to the relative size of the radio source. The accompanying illustration shows the resulting fringe pattern when the angular diameter of the source is smaller than the width of the individual lobes. Also shown is the resulting fringe pattern when the incoming signal is larger than the width of individual lobes.

A problem arises with this type of interferometer when it is used to receive signals from an area where a large "total power" signal is present. If the telescope is pointed toward the Milky Way, for example, there are several sources present, but they are absorbed by the large overall signal from the Milky Way itself.

THE PHASE-SWITCHING INTERFEROMETER

One solution to this problem is the *phase-switching interferometer*. The main difference between the phase-switched interferometer and the one just described is the addition of a phase-reversal switch in one of the transmission lines from one antenna.

The circuit operates as follows. With the switch in the open position, the signal output shown by the solid line is produced. In the closed-switch position, the phase is reversed, and the pattern indicated by the dotted line is produced. In the practical phase-switched interferometer, the phase switching is done electronically rather than with a hand-operated switch.

The signals from the two antennas are fed to the receiver. The phase reversal switch adds an additional half wavelength of transmission line which is shorted out about 60 times a second. A half-wave section of transmission line will provide a 180° phase reversal.

FRINGE PATTERN PRODUCED BY THE INTERFEROMETER

INTERFEROMETER OUTPUT FOR DIFFERENT SOURCES

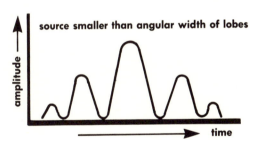

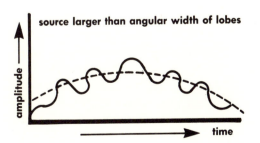

PHASE-SWITCHING INTERFEROMETER

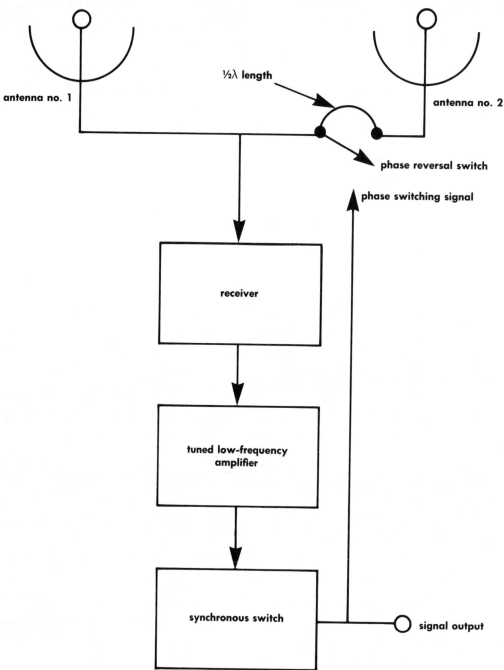

The receiver's output will be proportional to the total signal received at both antennas in the open-switch position, and to the difference between signals in the closed-switch position. The total signal power component will be equal for both switch positions and will thus cancel out. As shown in the resulting chart recording, the small signal sources are now much more visible.

THE MILLS CROSS

While most radio astronomy observations deal with wavelengths in the centimeter range, there is still considerable interest in the longer wavelengths of 0.1 meters or less. Certain sources in the Milky Way, as well as our sun, emit large amounts of radiation down to 0.1 meter.

OUTPUT SIGNAL FROM PHASE-SWITCHING INTERFEROMETER

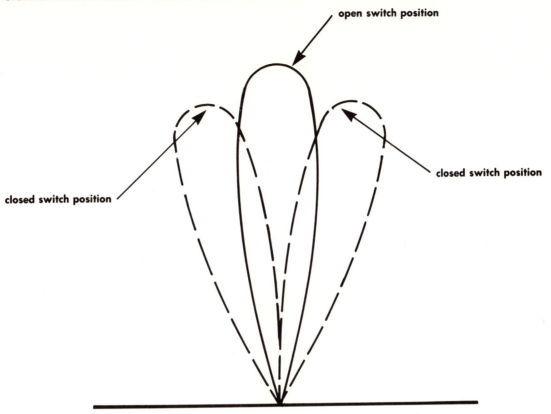

SMALL SIGNALS MORE VISIBLE WITH PHASE-SWITCHING INTERFEROMETER

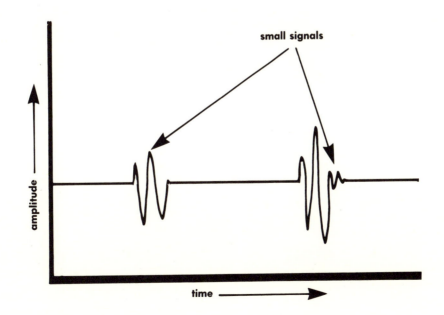

THE MILLS CROSS ANTENNA

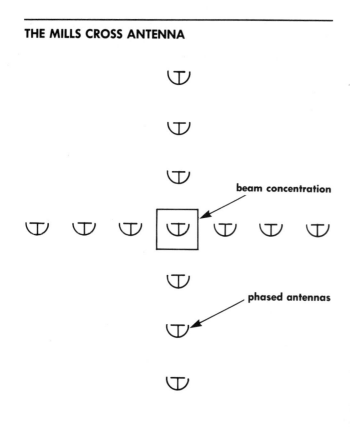

While there are several approaches for the reception of these long wavelengths involving collinear antennas and multielement beam antennas, a novel approach is the Mills Cross. From the illustration you can see that the system consists of a number of dipole antennas all pointed in the same direction. With proper phasing of these individual antennas, it is possible to obtain a very narrow "pencil-beam" receiving lobe. The major problem with the Mills Cross is the large amount of real estate required for its setup. One example of the Mills Cross is installed in Sydney, Australia. Each arm of the cross consists of 500 half-wave dipoles each extending for 1,500 feet.

THE KRAUS ANTENNA

Another interesting antenna configuration is the Kraus antenna, which is located at Ohio State University. Incoming radio signals first strike the tiltable flat reflector. From this point the signals are passed to the fixed parabolic reflector and from there to the receiver's antenna feed horn. A large metallic ground plane extends between the tiltable reflector and the parabola.

THE KRAUS ANTENNA

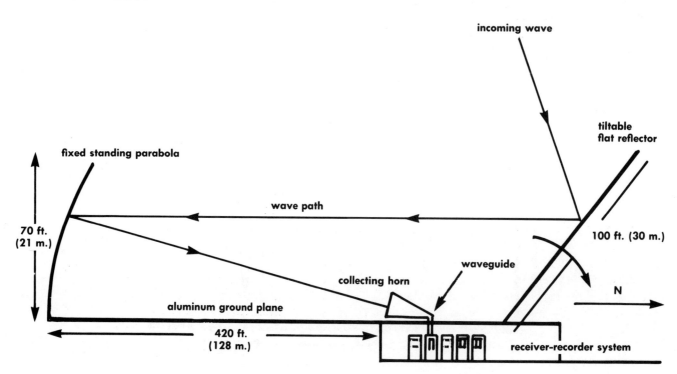

Basic Radio Astronomy Systems

THE DICKE RADIO TELESCOPE

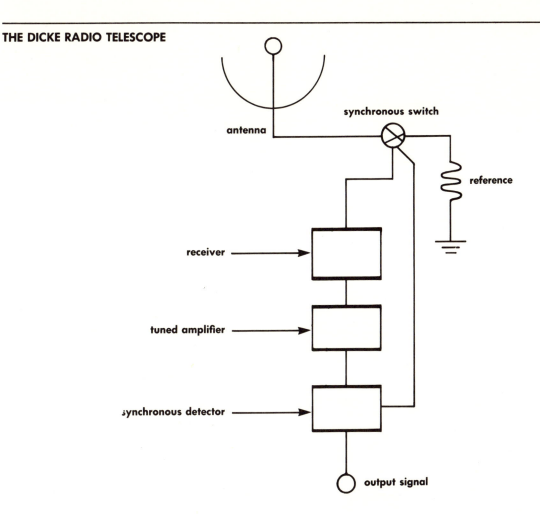

THE DICKE SYSTEM

As you will learn, one problem with radio telescope systems is receiver "noise." This internally generated noise tends to mask the desired incoming radio signal.

Illustrated is one solution to the problem, the Dicke system. Unlike the interferometer, which employs two antennas, the Dicke system employs only one antenna. The Dicke system operates by continuously comparing the signal arriving at the antenna with that from a fixed-voltage reference source. If the signal from the antenna is greater than the reference voltage, an output signal will be generated. The amplitude of this signal will be proportional to the difference between the two signals (antenna and reference). The resulting signal is amplified by a low-frequency amplifier. The output from the tuned amplifier is applied to the synchronous detector, which produces an output signal, which in turn is applied to the readout device.

One problem with the Dicke system is that the antenna is connected to the receiver only 50% of the time. As a result, the average output from the antenna is less than for a conventional single-antenna radiometer. However, this shortcoming is compensated for by the great decrease in receiver noise.

The Dicke system is most effective at the higher radio frequencies, UHF and microwave, where receiver noise is a problem. At VHF frequencies and lower atmospheric noise is more significant than receiver noise.

THE CLIFF INTERFEROMETER

The cliff interferometer was one of the earliest types developed. The system makes use of a body of water and a cliff for its operation. The incoming radio signal takes two paths, one directly to the antenna and the other first to the water and then to the antenna.

THE 1,000-FOOT ARECIBO TELESCOPE

Basic Radio Astronomy Systems

THE CLIFF INTERFEROMETER

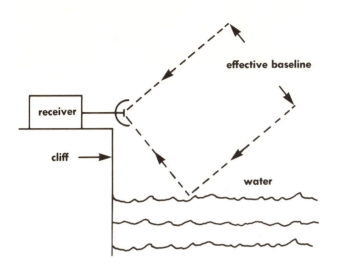

THE 1,000-FOOT ARECIBO ANTENNA

The 1,000-foot-diameter radio telescope built by Cornell University and situated in Puerto Rico is the largest of its type in the world. The antenna reflector uses a natural depression in the earth, covered with wire mesh, to serve as a reflective surface.

The steerable antenna is suspended from a large support structure, and steering is possible up to 20 degrees from the zenith. The antenna's large size makes it capable of receiving an extraordinarily wide range of wavelengths.

It is interesting to note that this telescope is being used "in reverse," transmitting powerful radio signals into the cosmos in the hope of contacting extraterrestrial civilizations. Also, its radar signals are being used to investigate the ionosphere.

7 The Radio Telescope Antenna

The antenna is perhaps the most important device in the entire radio telescope signal-receiving chain. The antenna gathers weak incoming radio waves and converts them into a corresponding electrical signal. We will examine the various types of radio telescope antennas and signal transmission lines that connect the antenna to the receiver. Let's first review the characteristics of the radio signal.

CHARACTERISTICS OF RECEIVED RADIATION

In optical astronomy, we use various units of light measurement, such as *lux*, *lumens*, *stardoms*, etc., to determine the intensity of the optical source. In radio astronomy, we also have means of determining the intensity of radiation.

The most commonly used measurements for this purpose are flux density, brightness, and brightness temperature. In general, radio astronomers prefer to use flux density units. The *flux density* is defined as the energy per unit of bandwidth falling on one unit of area in one unit of time. If we receive so many joules (a unit of energy) on an area of so many square meters in a fixed period of time using a receiving system with a frequency of so many hertz, then the flux density, S, can be expressed as follows:

$$S = \frac{E}{A \times F \times A}$$

where: S = flux density in watt-seconds
E = energy in joules
A = area in square meters
F = frequency in hertz
T = time in seconds

Flux densities for several typical radio sources, at a frequency of 400 MHz, are:

Cassiopeia A	6,000
Cygnus A	4,500
Hydra A	133
Taurus A	1,200
Virgo A	600

Brightness Temperature

Another measurement used in radio astronomy is *brightness temperature*. This concept makes use of Planck's Law, which describes the emission of electromagnetic energy in all frequencies from a black body, which is dependent on its temperature. Approximation of the law for radio frequencies is given as follows:

$$B = \frac{2KT}{\lambda^2}$$

where: B = brightness temperature
T = temperature in degrees Kelvin
λ = wavelength
K = Boltzmann's constant

This formula is usually used to determine the thermal radiation from an extraterrestrial source such as our sun.

THE GENERAL PROPERTIES OF AN ANTENNA

The fundamental purpose of an antenna is to convert the electromagnetic radiation striking it into a corresponding electrical signal. This is the case whether the antenna is a simple dipole or a 100-foot dish. All antennas can be evaluated in terms of the following: beamwidth, bandwidth, aperture, forward gain, front-to-back ratio, polarization, and impedance.

The *beamwidth* of an antenna is a measure of the narrowness of its receiving pattern. In the illustration, we see an antenna with a relatively wide beamwidth. Because of its wide beamwidth, it cannot distinguish between several discrete extraterrestrial radio sources. If the antenna has a narrower beamwidth, it is possible to separate individual radio sources.

The beamwidth is measured in degrees of arc—20°, 10°, 5°, etc. Thus, a beamwidth of 2° is narrower than one of 10°. In general, the larger the antenna, the narrower its beamwidth. That is why it is desirable to have as large an antenna as possible.

Another important characterstic of an antenna is its *bandwidth*. By this we mean the range of frequencies the antenna can receive. It is desirable to have an antenna with a fairly wide bandwidth because extraterrestrial radio signals are essentially wideband "noise." The amount of signal power received is directly proportional to antenna bandwidth. The greater the bandwidth, the greater the noise "power" received.

The area, or *aperture*, of the antenna is also an important consideration. The larger the area, the greater the amount of signal gathered by the antenna. In general, for most large antennas, such as broadside and parabola antennas, the electrical area can be figured to be about 0.5–0.9 times the actual physical size.

Forward gain is also an important consideration. The main purpose of any antenna is to convert incoming signals into an electrical voltage that appears across the antenna terminals. The amount of electromagnetic energy captured and converted into a

ANTENNA SIGNAL RESOLUTION

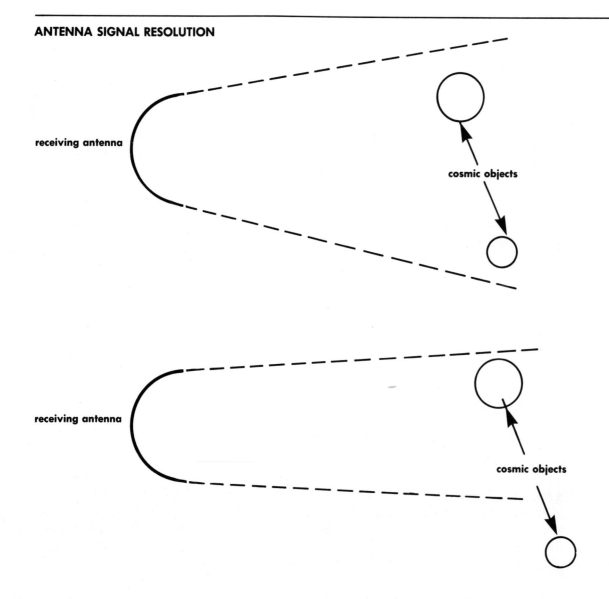

corresponding voltage is determined by the antenna's forward gain. The amount of forward gain is determined by the size of the antenna. The larger the antenna, the greater its forward gain. Forward gain is generally expressed as so many decibels over a standard reference, generally a half-wave dipole antenna mounted in free space. A 3- or 4-element TV-type antenna may have a gain of 4 or 5 decibels, whereas a large parabolic antenna may have a gain of 30 decibels or more.

The *front-to-back ratio* of an antenna is the ratio of signals picked up in the forward direction to those creeping in from the sides or back. It is necessary to have a good front-to-back ratio; otherwise unwanted stray signals and interference would be picked up by the antenna. As is the case with forward-gain antenna measurements, front-to-back ratios are calibrated in decibels.

Signal *polarization* is another significant antenna parameter. To clarify what we mean by polarization, remember that electromagnetic waves can be radiated in various planes. Antennas can be designed to have either horizontal or vertical polarization. Specialized antennas have been designed with circular polarizations.

The important thing to remember is that if a transmitter's radiated waves are horizontally polarized, little output will be obtained from a vertically polarized receiving antenna and vice versa. For maximum signal reception, both transmitting and receiving antennas must have the same polarization.

In most cases, extraterrestrial radio sources are randomly polarized, so either horizontal or vertical polarization may be used.

Another consideration is the electrical *impedance* of the antenna system. Simply put, impedance is AC resistance and is expressed in ohms. Ohm's Law can be used for determining impedance as follows:

$$I = \frac{E}{Z}$$
$$R = IZ$$
$$Z = \frac{E}{I}$$

where: I = current in amperes
E = volts
Z = impedance in ohms

The signals received from stellar objects will range anywhere from 50 KHz up through microwave frequencies. These are obviously AC signals, as they are so many millions of *cycles* per second.

Since the antennas are dealing with an AC signal, their termination is expressed as an impedance (Z) rather than in ohms (R).

The *termination* of the antenna is its effective output impedance, which may range from 75 to 300 ohms, depending on the particular antenna type. Additionally, for maximum signal-transfer efficiency, this antenna impedance must match the receiver's input impedance: 75-ohm antenna impedance to 75-ohm receiver impedance, for example.

The theory as to why antennas have specific termination impedances according to their design is beyond the scope of this book. The important thing to remember about antenna impedance is that it must be correctly matched to the radio telescope receiver unit.

TYPES OF RADIO TELESCOPE ANTENNAS

We will start our examination of the various types of radio telescope antennas with a description of the basic half-wave dipole, as it forms the basis for many other types of antennas.

The accompanying drawing shows the arrangement of the basic half-wave dipole antenna along with the voltage and current distribution along the length of the two elements. As you can see, the half-wave dipole consists of two elements half as long as the wavelength they are designed to receive. The center of these two elements is attached to a length of transmission line, which connects the antenna to the receiver. In operation, the incoming electromagnetic wave induces a current in the antenna elements as it passes through them. Remember, a varying electromagnetic wave will induce a current in a conductor through which it passes. The current at the center of the dipole is at a maximum, while the voltage at the center is at a minimum.

The half-wave antenna is known as a *resonant* antenna, and its element length is directly proportional to frequency. As the receiving frequency goes up, the antenna must become shorter. This is why your UHF TV antenna has shorter elements than does your VHF TV antenna—the higher the frequency, the shorter the antenna.

BASIC HALF-WAVE ANTENNA

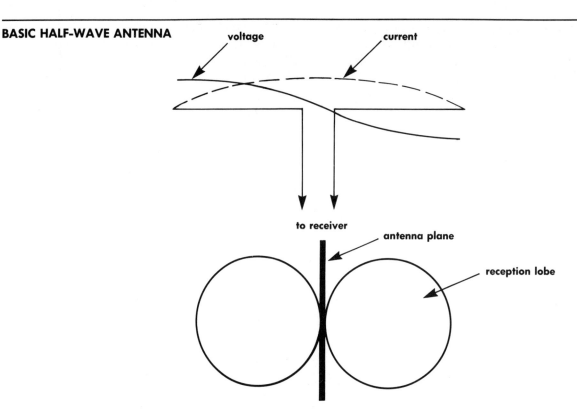

The length of a half-wave antenna can be determined by the following formula:

Antenna length (in feet) = $\dfrac{468}{\text{frequency (MHz)}}$

To see how this formula is applied, let us work an example. What is the length of a 7-MHz half-wave resonant dipole? The answer is:

$$L = \frac{468}{F} = \frac{468}{7} = 66 \text{ feet}$$

Let us try another example. The half-wave element for a radio telescope antenna is to be operated at 150 MHz. What is the length of the dipole element?

$$L = \frac{468}{150} = 3.12 \text{ feet}$$

From the above examples, it is clear that as the frequency goes up, the length of the antenna elements goes down.

Dipole Field Radiation Pattern

The accompanying illustration shows the signal reception pattern of the half-wave dipole. In the case of the half-wave dipole, the receiving pattern extends equally on both sides of the antenna. The signal is most intense at the ends of the antenna.

The Folded Dipole

The radiation pattern of the folded dipole is the same as that of the half-wave dipole, the one exception being that the folded dipole has a higher output impedance, namely 300 ohms. The termination impedance of an antenna has no bearing on its performance. However, the impedance must be properly matched to the input of the telescope amplifier.

Adding a Reflector

The half-wave dipole antenna has an omnidirectional pattern. It receives signals from both of its sides. If a reflector element is added behind the dipole antenna, the rear pattern will be canceled and the front pattern will be extended. It is much the same idea as placing a reflector behind a light bulb. The reflector directs all the light in the same direction. In this arrangement, the dipole antenna itself is called the *driven element*, while the element behind the driven element is termed the *reflector*.

The Radio Telescope Antenna

ADDING A REFLECTOR TO DECREASE ANTENNA BEAMWIDTH

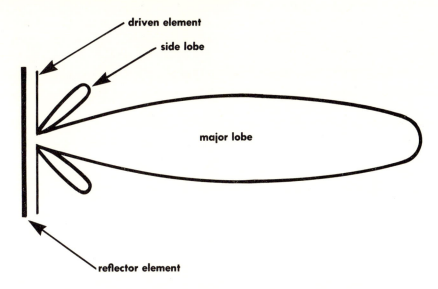

ADDING DIRECTOR ELEMENTS TO INCREASE ANTENNA GAIN AND DECREASE BEAMWIDTH

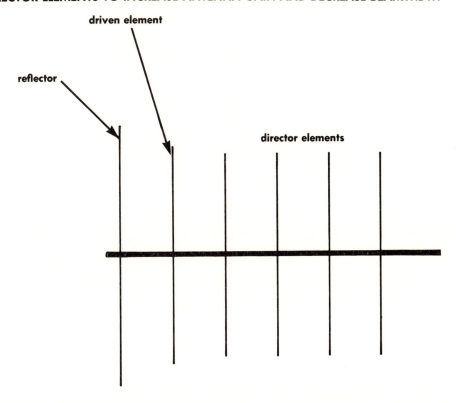

The driven element on any antenna is the point where the signal is taken from the antenna, i.e., the antenna terminal. In all cases, the reflector element is longer than the driven element. There are several reasons for adding a reflector. The gain of the antenna is increased and the beamwidth is slightly narrowed.

Adding Directors to the Antenna

The forward gain can be increased still further by adding *director elements* in front of the driven element. These director elements reinforce the signal being received by the antenna. The beamwidth is decreased still further and the gain increased as additional directors are added. However, a point of diminishing returns is reached where little improvement is gained with additional directors. A practical maximum number is about 12 directors.

No antenna, with the exception of the dish, has a perfect front-to-back ratio. There will always be some radiation around the sides and ends of the antenna. However, a well-designed antenna will have a large front-to-back ratio (this includes side lobes) of about 30 to 1.

The Collinear Antenna

The collinear antenna was used in the early days of radio astronomy for the study of extraterrestrial signals in the range of 50–200 MHz. Among its advantages are a wide bandwidth and aperture. Its beamwidth is determined by the number of elements employed.

The collinear antenna consists of a number of half-wave dipoles built up into a large array, backed

ARRANGEMENT OF THE COLLINEAR ANTENNA

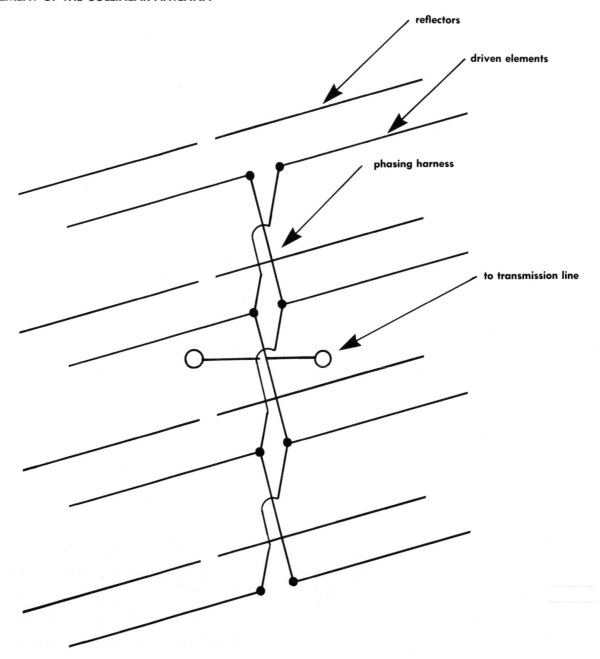

The Radio Telescope Antenna

ARRANGEMENT OF THE CORNER REFLECTOR ANTENNA

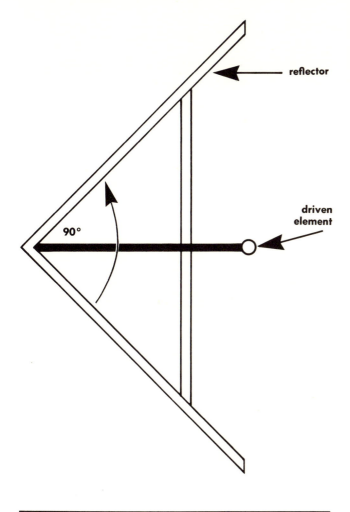

THE PARABOLOID ANTENNA

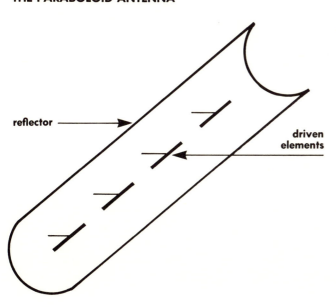

up by corresponding reflector elements. The collinear antenna is sometimes referred to as a "billboard" antenna, due to its large, flat size. Incidentally, the collinear antenna is an excellent antenna for the amateur radio astronomer, as it is easy to assemble and will provide good results.

The Corner Reflector Antenna

The corner reflector consists of two plane reflectors at a 90° angle and a half-wave dipole used as the driven element. For optimum performance, the reflector sides of the antenna should be at least several wavelengths long. From this, you can see that the corner reflector has to be quite large at lower frequencies.

The approximate gain of the corner reflector is about 12 decibels with a 90° angle. The amount of gain will vary with the angle.

The Paraboloid Antenna

A rather unusual antenna configuration is the paraboloid. This reflector is shaped in a parabolic curve that has the appearance of a trough. The driven elements consist of three half-wave antennas and are mounted at the reflector's focal point.

The physical construction of the paraboloid antenna is more critical than that of the corner antenna. The paraboloid reflector must be accurate to within one-eighth of a wavelength at all points. The paraboloid antenna is used in solar observations, where it is desirable to have a wide horizontal beamwidth.

The Space Age Helical Antenna

Invented by Dr. John Kraus of Ohio State University, the helical antenna has the unique property of having circular polarization.

The antenna consists of a "corkscrew" driven element, backed up by a metallic reflector. The reflector should be at least one-half wavelength per side. At lower frequencies, the reflector is often made up from wire screening, properly braced. At higher frequencies a solid metal reflector may be used, because of the shorter wavelengths at the higher frequencies. Remember, the higher the frequency, the shorter the antenna.

Each turn of the helix is 1 wavelength in circumference, and generally 8 to 10 turns are employed. The gain of the helix is between 12 and 14 decibels,

THE HELIX ANTENNA

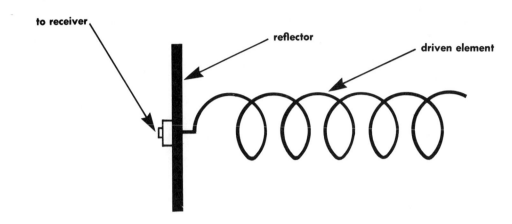

THE PARABOLIC ANTENNA

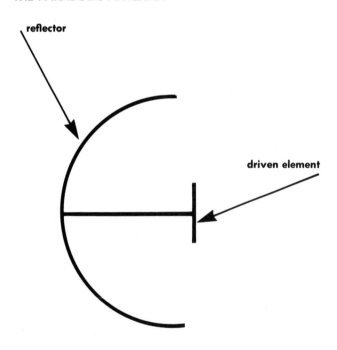

depending on the number of turns in the helix. The number of turns in the helix also has an effect on the antenna's beamwidth. The helix antenna is generally used for VHF and UHF applications.

The Parabolic Antenna

The parabolic antenna is perhaps the most widely used antenna in professional radio astronomy. It consists of a parabolic reflector element, with a half-wave dipole antenna mounted at its focal point.

For maximum gain, the reflector should be at least 10 wavelengths in diameter at the operating frequency. As a result, parabolic antennas are not generally used much below 1,000 MHz. The lower the frequency, the longer the wavelength and the larger the required antenna.

As an example of the size required for the parabolic antenna's reflector, let us say we wish to design a "dish" for operation at 500 MHz. This is a wavelength of 0.5 meters. Multiply this by 10 and we get a 5-meter diameter for the reflector—quite large!

One mechanical difficulty with the parabolic antenna is the very close tolerance on the reflecting surface. It must not vary by more than a quarter wavelength at its operating frequency.

Advantages of the parabolic antenna include a very high front-to-back ratio, a clean forward pattern, a high gain, and a simple driven-element feed system. The accompanying photo shows a parabolic antenna used by the Naval Research Laboratory.

COUPLING THE ANTENNA TO THE RECEIVER

The output terminals from the antenna must be connected to the radio telescope's receiver. One of the most important considerations is that the impedance of the antenna output match that of the receiver input. For example, if the antenna output impedance is 300 ohms, then the receiver input should also be 300 ohms. Similarly, if the antenna has an output impedance of 75 ohms, then the receiver should also have an input impedance of 75 ohms. Remember, for maximum energy transfer in any electrical circuit, the input and output impedance must be matched.

THE PARABOLIC ANTENNA

Transmission Lines

At receiving frequencies of 1,000 MHz and below, a parallel wire or coaxial cable is used to convey the signal from the antenna terminals to the receiver. At microwave frequencies, waveguides are generally used because of their lower energy loss as compared to conventional cable.

In a sense, the transmission lines are as important as the antenna itself, as any signal loss in the cable will reduce the amount of signal applied to the receiver.

In choosing a transmission line, certain characteristics of the line must be taken into consideration. Open-line transmission lines offer the least signal attenuation and would therefore appear to be the best choice. Open-line transmission line consists of two parallel wires spaced about 3 inches apart. Insulated "spreaders" placed at intervals along the wires keep the line separated at the correct spacing. The virtue of the open-line transmission line is that there is very little insulating material between the two conductors. Remember, the less insulation, the less signal loss. However, if the transmission line is to be exposed to areas of high electrical interference, this would degrade the received signal. Thus, in cases of high electrical interference, a better choice would be coaxial cable.

Coaxial cable is available in a number of impedances and energy-loss factors. In general, the larger the diameter of the cable, the lower its loss. The cable's inner dielectric material also has an effect on the amount of signal attenuation.

Cable Connectors

Another important consideration is the type of connector that joins the ends of the transmission line to the antenna and receiver terminals.

Inexpensive connectors that are poorly made can make poor electrical contacts, with resultant signal loss. By the same token, improperly fitted connectors can also cause a problem. I don't put too much faith in some of the new "solderless" connectors. You can't beat a good soldered connector.

ANTENNA MOUNTING

Another consideration is the proper mounting for the antenna. Since the antenna can be mounted close to the ground, the problem of tower mounting can be avoided. The only point to remember in this respect is that the lowest element must not be any closer to the ground than a half wavelength of the receiving frequency.

The reason for this limitation is that below a half wavelength, the termination impedance of the antenna will change drastically. This will decrease the efficiency of the antenna, which will deliver less output signal.

Generally, the antenna can be mounted in a fixed position, pointing due south. If solar observations are to be made, the antenna's elevation can be adjusted for the different heights of the sun during the various seasons.

8 Radio Telescope Receivers

The purpose of the radio telescope receiver is to amplify extremely weak extraterrestrial radio signals sufficiently to operate the readout device.

BASIC RECEIVER REQUIREMENTS

The basic radiometer radio telescope consists of an antenna, a receiver, and a signal readout device, such as a strip chart recorder.

One of the major problems with any radio telescope is that of electrical "noise," which will interfere with the incoming radio signal. The accompanying illustration is a curve showing the principal sources of noise in a radio telescope system. Below about 50 MHz, we find atmospheric noise, thunderstorms, and man-made electrical interference that mask the desired signal. However, as we attempt to detect higher frequencies, internally generated receiver noise becomes the main problem.

At any temperature above absolute zero, (−273° C), there is molecular motion in all materials. As the temperature goes up, so does the rate of molecular motion. In electrical conductors and semiconductors, this molecular motion causes a small amount of noise to be generated. The technical term for this phenomenon is *thermal agitation*, or simply thermal noise. The amplitude of this thermal noise increases as the temperature increases. While the amplitude of this noise is very small, it becomes significant in the very high gain amplifiers used in radio astronomy. Certain types of precision electronic devices are chilled to reduce the generation of thermal noise within them. Many professional radio astronomers employ what is called a *parametric amplifier* to boost very weak signals. In

PRINCIPAL SOURCES OF NOISE IN THE RADIO TELESCOPE SIGNAL

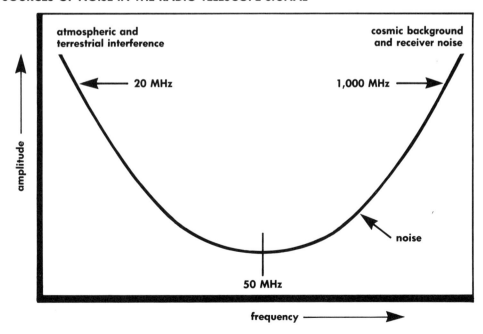

order to reduce the noise of the parametric amplifier to the lowest possible level, it is placed in liquid nitrogen, which has a temperature of nearly absolute zero. As a result, molecular motion, with its accompanying noise, is reduced to a minimum.

While professional radio astronomers use parametric amplifiers to obtain the lowest possible noise, the radio sources that the amateur is capable of receiving have signals strong enough so that inexpensive amplifiers can be used.

Noise and Bandwidth

It is desirable to have a wide bandwidth amplification system. Unfortunately, as the bandwidth is increased, so is the amplifier's internally generated noise. As a result, amplifier designers strike a compromise between gain and bandwidth.

The accompanying illustration shows the effect of noise on the received signal. The internally generated noise can mask the desired signal.

EFFECT OF INTERNALLY GENERATED RECEIVER NOISE

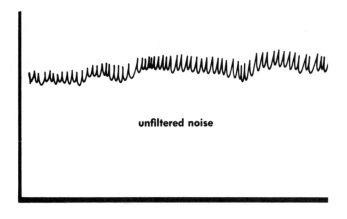

unfiltered noise

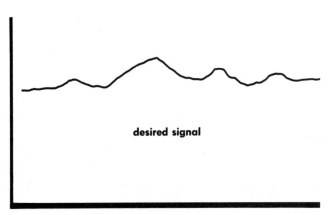

desired signal

RECEIVER TYPES

The *superheterodyne* receiver is the most commonly used type of receiver in radio astronomy. The receiver consists of an RF amplifier, mixer, local oscillator, intermediate frequency amplifier, detector/integrater, and output stage.

While there are other types of receivers, such as the *tuned radio frequency* (TRF) receiver, the superheterodyne receiver has the advantage that a high input frequency, UHF for example, can be converted to a lower frequency. This is beneficial because low-frequency amplifiers can be designed with higher gain or amplification and less noise than corresponding UHF amplifiers. Another advantage of the superheterodyne receiver is that the major part of the signal amplification occurs at a single frequency, called the *intermediate* frequency. Using a single IF frequency it is not necessary to retune the amplifier for changes in incoming signal frequency. Remember, in the superheterodyne receiver, all input frequencies are heterodyned to the same IF frequency.

THE SUPERHETERODYNE RF AMPLIFIER STAGE

The antenna output is fed to the RF amplifier, which serves two purposes: It amplifies the signal between the antenna and mixer stages, and it increases the receiver's signal-to-noise ratio. Signal-to-noise ratio is the ratio of internally generated receiver noise to the desired signal to be amplified. A high signal-to-noise ratio simply means that the amplified signal will be large in comparison to the internally generated noise signal.

The specific requirements of the RF amplifier include high signal-to-noise ratio, adequate bandwidth, freedom from spurious signal interference, relatively high signal gain, and freedom from amplitude variations.

One problem that must be avoided in the design of an IF amplifier is that of spurious signal generation. Specifically, spurious signals are produced when the amplifier goes into spontaneous oscillation at certain frequencies when an input signal is applied. A carefully designed and adjusted RF amplifier will avoid this problem.

Obviously, it is desirable to have as much signal gain as possible. The limiting factor is that excessive

THE SUPERHETERODYNE RECEIVER

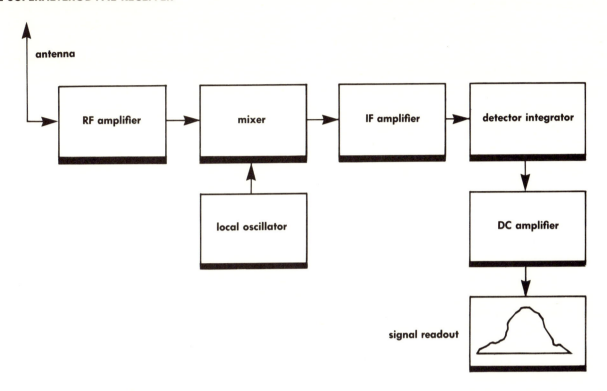

gain can lead to problems of amplifier instability.

Finally, the amplifier must be free of amplitude variations. Since we are dealing with a varying input signal, any internally caused amplifier drift would mask those variations.

THE MIXER STAGE

The mixer stage converts the higher frequency signal from the output of the RF amplifier to the lower intermediate frequency. The actual process is called the *heterodyne process*; hence the name superheterodyne receiver. In the heterodyne process, two signals are combined to form two additional frequencies. The output frequency from the RF amplifier is applied to the input of the mixer stage. The other input to the mixer stage is from the local oscillator, which generates an output frequency of 110 MHz. The mixing, or heterodyning action, of the 110-MHz local oscillator and the 140-MHz output signal from the RF amplifier produce two additional frequencies: 140 + 110 = 250 MHz and 140 − 110 = 30 MHz. You can see how the mixer can provide us with additional frequencies. In practice only one output frequency is selected; the others are filtered out. In this example, we would probably use the lower 30-MHz output.

THE HETERODYNE OSCILLATOR

There are several points that must be kept in mind in the design of the heterodyne oscillator. First, it must be free of frequency drift in its output signal. Any drift in frequency will be reflected as a shift in the resulting intermediate frequency. Second, the oscillator must be free of any spurious output signals.

Mixer-Stage Noise

The chief source of internally generated receiver noise is the heterodyne mixer. To minimize this noise, diode mixer stages, rather than transistors, are employed. Transistors are more "noisy," because the flow of the electric charges in them generates thermal noise. This noise is significantly less in diodes. Also, the addition of an RF amplifier stage before the mixer will help to reduce mixer noise, because then the mixer gain can be reduced, with a consequent reduction in noise.

THE INTERMEDIATE FREQUENCY (IF) AMPLIFIER

The IF amplifier receives one of the output frequencies from the mixer stage. It is the IF amplifier's job to provide the bulk of the amplification in the receiver, and as a result more than one amplifier stage is used. Most radio telescope IF amplifiers have a gain in excess of 70 decibels.

IF AMPLIFIER BANDWIDTH

The radio telescope receiver must have sufficient frequency bandwidth to adequately pass the wide band of frequencies necessary for maximum received signal power. In order to accomplish this, the IF amplifier stage also must have sufficient bandwidth.

There are several methods of obtaining the required wide bandpass on the IF amplifier. The first consists of placing "swamping" resistors across the windings of several of the amplifier's resonant-tuned circuits. These resistors will lower the effective Q of the resonant circuits, thus increasing their bandwidth. Generally speaking, the Q (quality factor) of a tuned (resonant) circuit determines its frequency selectivity.

The primary factors that determine the circuit Q are its associated electrical losses. These include resistance of the wire from which the coil is wound, dielectric losses in the resonant-circuit capacitor, and resistance in the resonant circuit at the connecting leads. The greater these losses, the lower the resonant circuit's Q. The formula for determining Q is as follows:

$$Q = \frac{X}{R}$$

where: Q = quality factor
X = reactance of either coil or capacitor
R = series resistance in ohms

The second method of increasing bandwidth is called *stagger tuning*. The several individual resonant circuits are each tuned to a slightly different frequency. The net effect is that their frequency response curves overlap, causing a nice broad and uniform overall frequency response. This arrangement has the advantage over "swamping" resistors, as these resistors decrease the gain of the amplifier, which often means that another amplifier stage must be added to make up the loss.

In radio telescope systems, the usual IF amplifier frequencies will range from 450 KHz to 30 MHz, depending on the receiving signal.

EFFECT OF Q ON BANDWIDTH OF RESONANT CIRCUITS

high Q resonant circuit–narrow bandpass

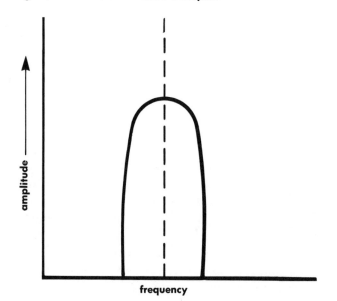

low Q circuit–wide bandpass

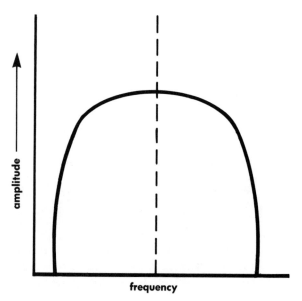

The Detector Stage

It is necessary to rectify the output signal from the IF amplifier to create a DC signal for application to the recorder. The output from the last IF amplifier stage is fed to a semiconductor diode. The rectified output signal from this diode detector is a varying DC voltage that is in step with the changing input signal from the antenna. This type of detector is called a *square law detector*, as it responds to the average power of the received signal.

The Integrator

The output from the diode is "rough," that is, consisting of large variations in average output. It is necessary to smooth out these variations to obtain an average waveform. This task is accomplished by the integrator network that follows the detector. This network consists of a series resistor and three capacitors. Three different values of capacitors are used so that differing integrator times can be had.

THE DC AMPLIFIER

The output from the integrator generally needs additional amplification before it is finally applied to the readout device. To this end, a DC amplifier is employed to boost the DC signal level.

THE CALIBRATING REFERENCE

The amplifier and other circuitry in the radio telescope system are subject to drift over time. Because of this drift, means must be provided to calibrate the output of the receiver to a known reference source.

The simplest reference source would involve a carbon composition 1-watt resistor of the same resistance as the antenna's impedance (75 ohms, e.g.), temporarily substituted for the antenna's output. The voltage level of the receiver is noted. The an-

EFFECT OF INTEGRATOR ON DETECTOR OUTPUT

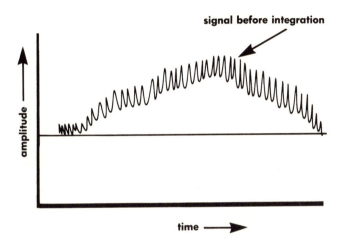

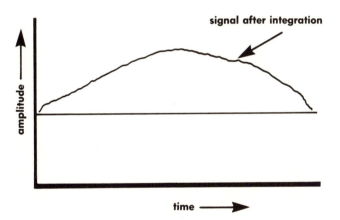

USING A CALIBRATION RESISTOR TO CHECK RECEIVER DRIFT

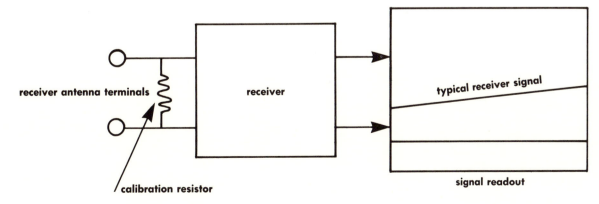

tenna is then switched back to the RF amplifier input, and any drift in the receiver will be detected.

READOUT DEVICES

The readout device is the end link in the radio telescope chain, and it has the task of converting the electrical signal into a corresponding physical readout.

The most commonly used readout is the strip chart recorder, which consists of a strip of paper drawn under a recording pen. By suitable means, the pen moves back and forth over the paper, leaving a line, or *trace*, at the point where it touches the paper. The paper is drawn past the pen at a slow speed, generally less than 1 inch per hour.

Audio Monitors

It is often desirable to listen to the incoming radio signals, particularly in the case of Jupiter, which produces very interesting surflike sounds.

In operation, the audio amplifier stage is connected to the output of the detector, before the R-C integrating network.

Computer Readout

The use of a computer makes for a much more sophisticated readout. Great amounts of data can be analyzed and stored in the computer's memory for future evaluation. Computer graphics are also used to a great extent in radio astronomy.

9 And Now into Practice

We will now turn our attention to the practical problems of assembling a radio telescope. As with any project, it is a good idea to first form a game plan as to just what we want to accomplish. A little time spent on preparation in the beginning will pay rich dividends in the completed project down the road.

WHAT IS THE BEST OPERATING FREQUENCY?

One of the most important questions the neophyte radio astronomer must ask is, What operating frequency should I use? Often the beginner, seeing these big parabolic dishes, decides that is the way to go. Actually, these dishes are meant for use at microwave frequencies of several GHz and up. The construction of these parabolic reflectors is very critical; their reflecting surfaces must be kept to a half-wavelength accuracy.

Even if the amateur radio astronomer had the money to buy a large microwave dish, there is also the problem of handling the received signals at these frequencies. Microwave technology is entirely different from the lower frequency "two-wire" antenna and transmission-line equipment. For example, waveguide replaces conventional two-wire or coaxial cable, and one gets into the use of parametric amplifiers, also a few thousand dollars each.

Don't be discouraged. The range of 17 KHz up through 400 MHz can be readily handled by the average experimenter, and very meaningful and useful experiments and observations can be made in this range of frequencies. It really depends on the type of observations you wish to make. For example, observations of solar activity, such as solar flares, are best carried out between 100 and 200 MHz, where the solar activity is most intense. If you are interested in the effect of the ionosphere on radio signal propagation, you will want to use a receiving frequency of between 20 and 100 KHz. If your interest lies in the detection of Jovian signals, then you will want to receive frequencies in the neighborhood of 18–22 MHz. If chasing meteors intrigues you, a standard, good-quality FM receiver and directional antenna will make an excellent meteor-shower counter. Finally, if you are interested in a detailed study of extraterrestrial radio sources, your best bet is a 400-MHz interferometer. From all this, you can see that you have a lot to choose from in the way of amateur radio projects.

SELECTING RADIO TELESCOPE COMPONENTS

Once you have decided which type of radio telescope system you want to assemble, the next step is to lay out the whole arrangement on paper. For example, you will want to list the type of antenna, receiver, preamplifier (if used), power supply, integrator, and readout device, along with all their interconnections. In a sense, you are making a construction blueprint for your project.

Getting the Parts

At present, you can't go down to your local electronics store and purchase a ready-made amateur radio telescope. As a result, you have to "roll your own." Generally, most of the components you will need can be obtained from your local electronics parts supplier, which can be found in your Yellow Pages. It's a good idea to request their parts catalogs, as generally you have to order the items you want by their catalog part numbers. Often the parts supplier will require a minimum purchase of $5 or so. The policy is stated in the catalog. In most of the larger cities there are electronics suppliers and military-surplus electronics stores that have a lot of goodies at reasonable prices. Some of these places are wonderlands of unusual but useful electronics parts and assemblies.

When you are building an antenna, which is assembled partly from wood, a good source is your local lumberyard. They are generally happy to cut the wood to your order.

In the case of RF preamplifiers, converters, IF strips, etc., I strongly recommend that you purchase them ready-made for several reasons. First, a great deal of time can be spent collecting all the parts, trying to etch a printed circuit board (VHF and UHF circuits should always be assembled on a PC board for stability), and wiring up and testing the unit. There are several manufacturers who offer VHF and UHF RF preamplifiers, converters, and IF amplifier strips at reasonable cost.

The RF amplifier, converters, and IF amplifier stages must be designed and adjusted for the lowest possible noise (high signal-to-noise ratio). Unless you have the proper test equipment, it's almost impossible to get a satisfactory noise level on a homemade unit. So here again it pays to buy a ready-made unit, where the manufacturer guarantees the unit's gain and noise figures.

There are of course many parts of your radio telescope that you can assemble yourself. For example, the detector/integrator is a noncritical circuit and can be easily assembled without fear of failure. The DC amplifier and calibrator can also be assembled without difficulty.

COMPONENT REQUIREMENTS

Let's look at the basic requirements of the various components in the system. One point I want to emphasize is that you should not skimp on the quality of the components, particularly in the case of the RF components (RF amplifier, converters, etc.). These components aren't too expensive anyway, so shoot for the best you can afford.

Antennas

In the case of antennas, you can either purchase them or build your own. One virtue of purchasing ready-made antennas, particularly for operation at 144 and 420 MHz, is that they are close to the amateur radio frequencies. These antennas are made in quantity and are inexpensive. I couldn't assemble a 15-element beam antenna as cheaply as I could buy a standard 2-meter amateur radio antenna.

Antenna Gain Requirements

The minimum usable antenna gain for the amateur radio telescope is about 10 decibels. Anything below this will not yield observable results. An antenna gain of about 10 decibels will be sufficient for the observation of major solar activity and large extended signals from the Milky Way. If you wish to

DETECTOR/INTEGRATOR CIRCUIT

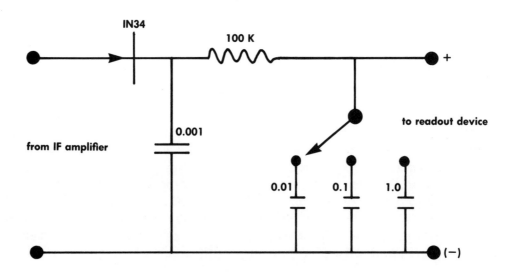

receive discrete radio sources, then you will need an antenna system of at least 15–18 decibels or better. One exception to this is in the reception of Jovian signals, which are so intense that a simple dipole antenna will generally be sufficient.

For reception of signals in the 140-MHz region, either beam antennas or quad antennas work well. You can purchase ready-made beam antennas for the 140-MHz range at any amateur radio store. These beam antennas come in a range of sizes and number of elements. Common element numbers are 7, 11, and 15, for a single-bay antenna. The 7-element beam antenna has a gain of around 8 decibels, the 11-element about 12 decibels, and the 15-element about 15–18 decibels. These are approximate figures; the exact figures will vary from manufacturer to manufacturer. The dealer can help you out on this. It is also possible to stack individual bays to increase the overall gain. In general, stacking will add about 3 decibels in total gain.

The quad antenna is another good choice for the 120–140-MHz band. The quad is easily built at home, using materials from a lumberyard and local hardware store. Element for element, the gain of the quad antenna is somewhat higher than that of a comparable beam antenna. Another advantage of the quad antenna is that it is polarized in both the horizontal and vertical planes. As a result, it will give a somewhat better performance for radio astronomy work, as extraterrestrial radio signals are randomly polarized.

The Helical Antenna

The helical antenna, or helix, is an antenna with a unique circular pattern. The approximate gain for an 8-turn helix at 140 MHz is about 12 decibels. One disadvantage of the helix at 140 MHz is that it is quite large; equal performance can be had with a smaller 11-element beam antenna.

The Collinear Antenna

Although very large, the collinear antenna can be either purchased or home-built, as it is simple in construction—just a bunch of half-wave dipoles backed up with an equal number of reflector elements. Collinear antennas are available for both 140 and 420 MHz from several manufacturers at reasonable prices. At 420 MHz, a pair of 20-element collinear antennas will make a good interferometer.

Receivers

The receiver must possess certain qualities, including high gain or amplification (at least 70 decibels), wide predetection bandwidth, high signal-to-noise ratio, low amplitude drift, and freedom from spurious output signals.

A good-quality FM tuner or receiver makes a good starting radio telescope receiver for the amateur. Most better quality FM receivers have reasonably high gain, particularly the newer solid-state units with MOSFET transistors in their "front ends." The predetection bandwidth of the average FM receiver is about 100 KHz, which is adequate for the beginner.

The better quality FM receivers have a reasonably good signal-to-noise ratio. Most of the better receiver manufacturers will list the noise response in their specs. The rating in decibels simply indicates the ratio of received signal to the noise generated within the receiver. The lower the number, the less the total noise.

As far as low-signal amplitude drift is concerned, just let the receiver warm up for about half an hour before making any measurements. Transistor receivers tend to be more stable than their vacuum-tube counterparts, as vacuum tubes create heat and consequent receiver drift.

Most of the FM receivers on the market are essentially free of any spurious output signals.

The Modular Approach

One method by which you can get the best receiving system for the money is the modular approach. This arrangement offers several advantages.

First, several manufacturers offer RF amplifiers, converters, IF amplifier stages, etc., at reasonable prices. As a result, a total receiver of better overall performance can be had for less than a comparable FM unit. You also save by not paying for the frills of a complete FM receiver—audio section, speaker, etc.

Second, the IF amplifier, strip detector, integrator, and DC output amplifier are the same, regardless of the receiving frequency. To change the receiving frequency, just change the RF amplifier and converter stages. Since these prepackaged IF amplifiers and converters have their own specific input and output wiring, follow their instruction sheets when changing modules. Generally, it just involves a desoldering operation.

THE MODULAR APPROACH FOR RADIO TELESCOPE ASSEMBLY

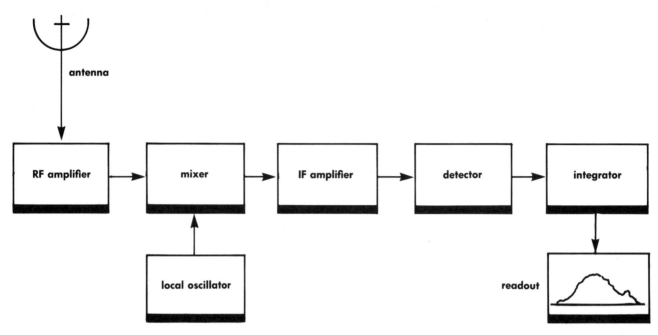

To see how this modular arrangement works, let us say you wish to assemble a 144-MHz radiometer for solar observations. All you do is insert a 144-MHz RF amplifier and converter. You now have a complete 144-MHz receiver. Let's say you want to make up a 400-MHz interferometer. All you have to do is substitute a 400-MHz RF amplifier and converter in place of the 140-MHz units. Everything else stays the same.

MECHANICAL ASSEMBLY

One of the most important points in the assembly of the telescope is its mechanical integrity. Many a beginner will design an excellent radio telescope on paper, only to wind up with marginal results due to poor mechanical assembly. Often the enthusiastic amateur will overlook proper component assembly procedures and practices. There are a number of points that must be taken into consideration if you are to obtain smooth operation of your telescope.

When assembling the various components, make sure that all the various nuts and lock washers are secure. Another point often overlooked is the proper assembly of the RF cable connectors. *Do not use those new solderless RF connectors, such as solderless PL-259 coaxial plugs.* It's been my experience that the internal connections often will work loose and thus degrade performance. If you are using several component assemblies, it is a good idea to mount them all together on a piece of plywood or some other rigid support.

Another point that is often overlooked is that of proper grounding and shielding. There is a tremendous amount of signal amplification between the input of the radio telescope and the recorder, generally in excess of 70 decibels. If proper shielding and grounding are not employed, strong signals will leak through, causing instability and, in severe cases, circuit oscillations.

One method of providing good shielding when you are using separate RF amplifiers, converters, etc., is to mount the circuit boards in a small minibox. These boxes are available in a wide variety of sizes and shapes. The circuit board is spaced away from the bottom of the box by means of small stand-off insulators. DC operating power leads and the on-off switch are mounted, and the input and output RF connectors are brought out to opposite ends of the box.

Another problem is proper power supply decoupling. A small capacitor is connected between the positive lead of each unit and the ground. The value of this capacitor is not particularly critical; any value from 0.01 to 0.11 MF will be satisfactory. The connecting leads from these capacitors should be as short and direct as possible.

USING A SHIELDED ENCLOSURE

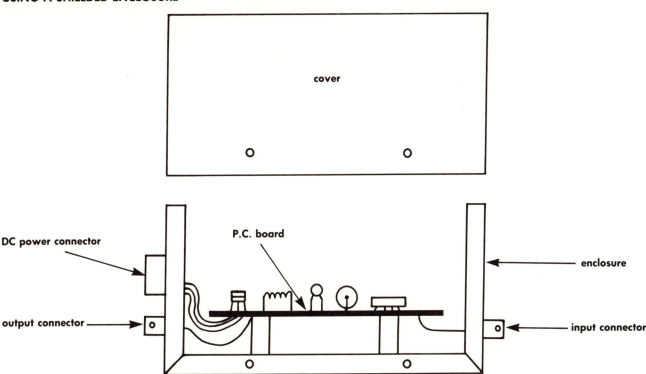

Grounding

A good, solid ground should be provided for all the units in the system. The cold-water plumbing line in your house will make an excellent ground, or you can use a ground rod, available from most hardware and electrical supply houses. Be sure to keep the lead from your equipment to the ground as short as possible. Also, use at least 16-gauge or larger wire.

POWER SUPPLIES

If you are purchasing separate RF amplifiers, mixers, and IF amplifier strips, you will need a source of operating power for them. These units generally operate from a source of 12-volt DC. While you could assemble a suitable power supply, it is cheaper to purchase one ready-made. It is important that the power supply be voltage regulated, as variations in its output voltage will be reflected as an amplitude variation in the signal from the telescope.

Power Line Interference

Another problem faced by the experimenter is radio frequency interference from the 60-Hz power line feeding the radio telescope units. This problem becomes more severe at the lower receiving frequencies. One method of eliminating this problem is to install a power line interference filter between the power line and the input to the radio telescope's power supply. Power line filters are available from most electronics supply stores. If you wish to build your own filter, the schematic for a satisfactory unit is shown in the accompanying illustration.

POWER LINE INTERFERENCE FILTER

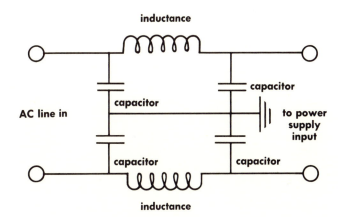

GOOD HOUSEKEEPING

One final point that I want to make is the importance of proper equipment "housekeeping."

When assembling homemade equipment, be sure to use lock washers under all mounting screws, to prevent them from loosening up due to vibration, etc. I've had instances where a grounding wire under a screw loosened up just enough to cause intermittent circuit operation.

Another problem is that of loose or corroded antenna connection terminals. Be sure to periodically check and clean all antenna terminals. To prevent corrosion, spread a thin layer of petroleum jelly over the exposed terminals once they are tightened.

A build-up of dust or dirt in or around the electronics of your telescope will often cause problems. The cure for this is a vacuum cleaner.

10 Antenna Design and Construction

We are going to take a look at some practical amateur radio telescope antennas.

THE BEAM ANTENNA

The beam antenna is one type of antenna that finds effective use in amateur radio astronomy. The antenna consists of a reflector, a driven element, and three directors.

The gain of the beam antenna is roughly proportional to the number of director elements. The more directors, the greater the antenna gain. However, a point of diminishing returns is reached, after which adding additional elements has little effect. For most beam antennas, about 15 elements are the maximum. The beamwidth is also decreased when the number of director elements is increased.

While it is possible to build your beam antenna, I recommend that you purchase it ready-made. The physical dimensions of the beam antenna are rather critical. Several manufacturers offer 140-MHz beam antennas at less than you would pay for the materials yourself, and the manufacturers will guarantee the specifications of their antennas.

THE QUAD ANTENNA

One of my favorite antennas is the quad antenna. As shown in the accompanying illustration, it consists mainly of "sticks and wire," and it is easy to construct on your own. The dimensions are not as critical as with the beam antenna, and the materials are inexpensive and easy to obtain.

As with the beam antenna, the gain of the quad will increase as you increase the number of director elements. It is interesting to note that, element for element, the gain of the quad is a bit higher than that of the beam antenna. For example, a 7-element quad will have about the same gain as a 10-element beam antenna.

Quad Antenna Construction Details

Each side of the driven element of the quad is one-quarter wavelength. As a result, the total circumference of the loop will be a full wavelength at the receiving frequency. Using the formula for a frequency of 144 MHz:

$$\text{Length (in meters)} = \frac{300}{\text{Frequency (in MHz)}}$$
$$= \frac{300}{144} = 2 \text{ meters} = 80 \text{ inches}$$

Thus, each side of the quad will be 20 inches $\left(\frac{80}{4} = 20\right)$

The reflector element is 5% larger around than the driven element. Thus at 144 MHz, the reflector element would be:

$$80 \times 0.05 = 4 \text{ inches}$$
$$80 + 4 = 84 \text{ inches}$$

By the same token, the director elements are 5% shorter than the driven element. Thus, at 144 MHz, the first director element would be:

$$80 \times 0.05 = 4 \text{ inches}$$
$$80 - 4 = 76 \text{ inches}$$

Going further, each director is 5% shorter than the previous director. The second director is:

$$76 \times 0.05 = 72 \text{ inches}$$

SEVEN-ELEMENT QUAD ANTENNA

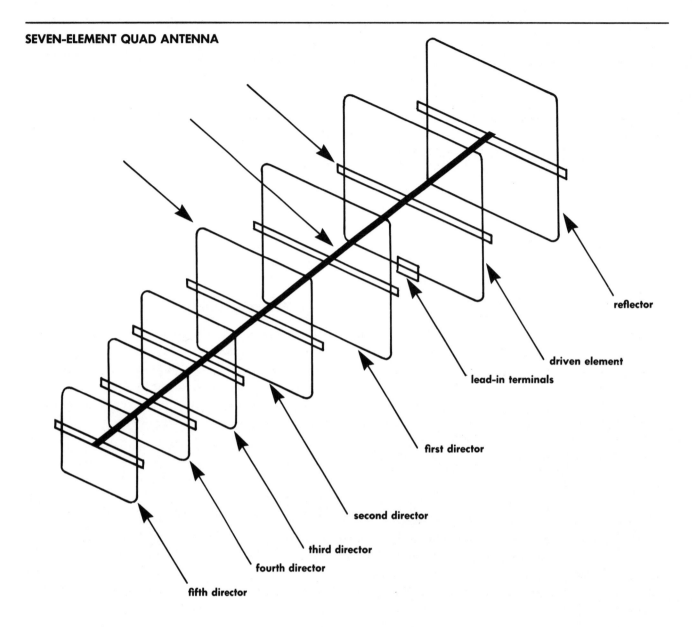

Notice that we rounded off the exact figure. If you make each director 4 inches shorter than the previous one, this will be close enough. The exact dimensions of the quad are not that critical.

The wire elements for the antenna can be either solid aluminum clothesline wire or #4 or #6 solid aluminum guy wire. This material is easy to work with and can be easily formed into the square element shapes. The aluminum clothesline wire can be obtained at most larger hardware stores, and the aluminum guy wire is available at most electronics parts outlets. Since you can't solder aluminum, you can join the ends of the elements with crimp-on terminals.

The boom for the seven elements is made from 2-inch-x-1-inch lumber. When you buy this wood, you will find that you will get something closer to 1⅞ x ⅞. This is satisfactory.

The termination impedance of the quad is close to 75 ohms, so you can use standard RG8/U coaxial cable for the connection from the antenna to the receiver. I don't recommend the use of the smaller diameter coaxial cable, such as the RG/59U. Its dielectric losses are too great at the VHF frequencies.

The theoretical gain of this antenna is about 14 decibels. You can increase the gain by about 3 decibels by means of a 4-bay quad.

Antenna Design and Construction

A Larger Antenna

The 4-bay quad antenna shown in the accompanying illustration will give excellent performance and should have a gain of about 17 decibels. Another advantage of this antenna is its wide aperture, which will aid in its signal-gathering ability. Incidentally, a pair of these 4-bay quads will make an excellent interferometer at 144 MHz if you have enough space.

This 4-bay antenna consists of four of the 7-element quads arranged in a boxlike configuration. Since the termination impedance of each 7-element bay is 75 ohms and there are four bays, you must provide a correct impedance match for the four antennas. A wiring "harness" is made up from lengths of 300-ohm TV lead-in wire. The 0.75-wavelength sections of the 300-ohm line step up the impedance to 1,200 ohms. Paralleling these line sections will result in an impedance of 600 ohms. Two 1-wavelength sections of 300-ohm line are connected so as to halve the 600 ohms to 300 ohms. As a result, the final output impedance of the total antenna is 300 ohms.

THE HELICAL ANTENNA

The helical antenna's driven element consists of a wire spiral backed by a metal reflector. The design and construction of the helical antenna are not criti-

FOUR-BAY QUAD ANTENNA WIRING ARRANGEMENT

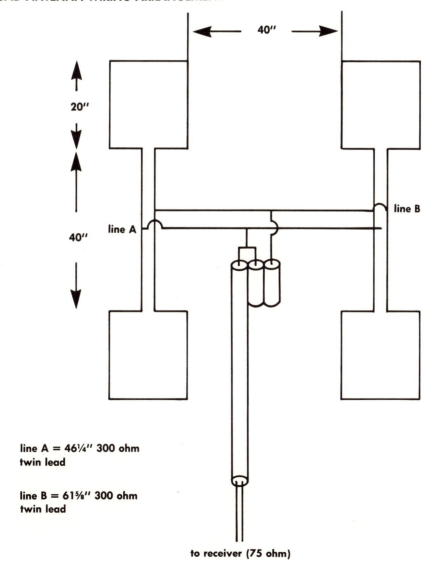

line A = 46¼" 300 ohm twin lead

line B = 61⅝" 300 ohm twin lead

to receiver (75 ohm)

THE HELIX ANTENNA

cal, and dimensions for the desired frequency can be calculated as follows:

1. Each turn in the spiral of the helix should have a circumference of 1 wavelength at the receiving frequency.
2. Spacing between adjacent turns should be 0.2 wavelengths at the receiving frequency.
3. The reflector must be at least 0.8 wavelengths per side at the receiving frequency.

To see how the above statements work out, let us consider the design of a helix antenna for 144 MHz. First, the circumference of each turn will be:

$$\frac{300}{144 \text{ (MHz)}} = 2 \text{ meters (approximately 80 inches)}$$

Spacing between adjacent turns = 0.3 × 80 inches = 16 inches

Reflector size = 0.8 wavelength per side = 80 inches per side at 144 MHz.

Because of the large size of the reflector at 144 MHz, it is more practical, and cheaper, to assemble the reflector out of aluminum window screen.

The termination impedance of the helix is about 140 ohms. However, the slight mismatch to 75-ohm coaxial cable will not be too much of a problem at 144 MHz.

The helix has a relatively low Q, and as a result will possess a fairly wide bandwidth. Also, as we mentioned earlier, the helix has a circular polarization pattern.

ANTENNA MOUNTINGS

One nice thing about the radio telescope antenna is that it does not have to be elevated very far above ground. In fact, up to a point, the closer to the ground the antenna, the less the terrestrial interference.

As far as the amateur radio astronomer is concerned, relatively simple antenna-mounting arrangements can be used. For example, the antenna

Antenna Design and Construction

STEPLADDER ANTENNA MOUNT

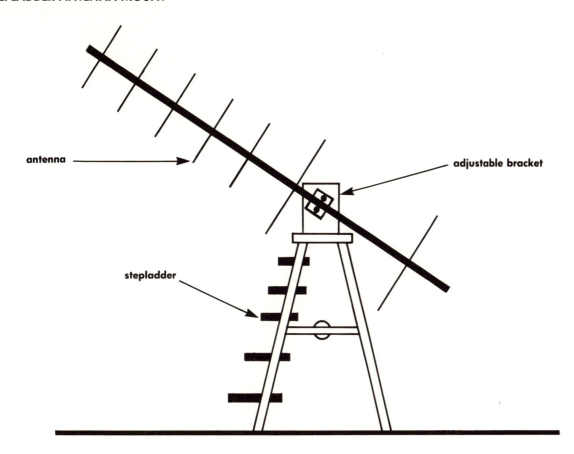

does not have to be rotated. Remember, the earth does the rotating, sweeping the antenna across the sky as it turns.

The accompanying illustration shows a novel arrangement that is satisfactory for mounting relatively lightweight antennas. A standard stepladder can be used for the antenna mount. The antenna is secured to the stepladder by a metal plate attached to the stepladder with L-brackets. The metal mounting bracket is notched so that the antenna's elevation can be changed. This is particularly useful when the antenna is used for solar observations, as the sun has differing elevations over the course of the year. This stepladder arrangement is also handy when two antennas are used in an interferometer setup. The mount for an amateur radio telescope does not have to be as rigid as that for an optical telescope.

11 Observing the Sun

The radio signals emitted by our sun are of great interest to the amateur radio astronomer for several reasons. First, because of the relatively high intensity of the signals, they are easy to receive on inexpensive equipment. Second, the output from the sun varies almost on a day-to-day basis, so there is always something new to listen to.

There are two basic means of measuring the sun's radio activity. In the *direct method,* the actual radio signals from the sun are detected by the radio telescope. In the *indirect method,* the effect of the sun's radiation on the earth's ionosphere is measured. Both these methods can be easily explored by the amateur radio astronomer.

A 108-MHz DIRECT SOLAR RADIO RECEIVER

The accompanying illustration shows the arrangement of the 108-MHz solar radiometer. The setup consists of the antenna, FM tuner/receiver, integrator, and readout device.

The Antenna

Because of the relatively high intensity of solar radiation, particularly solar flares, a large amount of antenna gain is not required. As a result, the 7-element quad antenna described in the previous chapter, modified for 108 MHz, will do the job.

Since this antenna is fairly lightweight, the stepladder mounting approach mentioned in the last chapter will suffice. If you use this arrangement, you should have several sets of mounting holes in the metal bracket that holds the antenna boom. This will allow you to change the antenna's elevation to compensate for differing heights of the sun during the year. In positioning the antenna, remember that its view should not be obstructed by trees, buildings, etc., and also that it should be pointed due south.

It is very important to use a low-loss transmission

SOLAR RADIOMETER

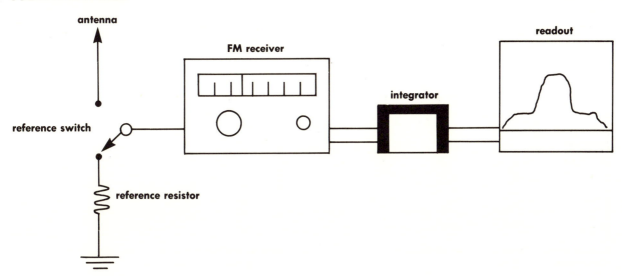

line between the antenna and the receiver. The antenna should have a 75-ohm termination impedance. Most commercial beam and collinear antennas have this impedance. I strongly suggest the use of good-quality RG8/U coaxial cable for the transmission line. The length of the transmission line from antenna to receiver should be as short and direct as possible, and be sure to use good-quality fittings on the cable.

The Receiver

An FM tuner or radio is used as the radio telescope receiver. There are several reasons for choosing an FM receiver for this project. First, the gain and the predetection bandwidth of even a modestly priced FM receiver or tuner are satisfactory for this solar radio telescope. Second, the modern solid-state FM units have relatively low-noise "front ends," so that internally generated noise won't be too much of a problem. The "front end" of a receiver is its first radio frequency amplifier stage, which amplifies the signal obtained from the antenna. Third, the FM units can be readily modified for the amateur radio telescope project without too much major surgery.

The Integrator

The purpose of the integrator network is to smooth out the small variations in the output of the detector stage and to provide an "average" output signal. Rapid signal variations are smoothed out as shown in the illustration. The integrator stage is nothing more than a resistor and three switch-selected capacitors.

The Readout Device

Depending on the size of your pocketbook, the readout device can be as simple as a 20,000-ohm/volt multimeter or a strip chart recorder. I do not recommend the use of a digital meter for the readout because of the nature of the received signal. You can't get a steady reading. The numbers jump all over the place.

You might consider approaching your local college or university with your project. Often they will either loan you a chart recorder or have a used one that you can buy at a reasonable price.

Incidentally, the Rustrak Company offers inexpensive strip chart recorders in the neighborhood of $150. I do recommend the use of a strip chart recorder if at all possible, as it greatly simplifies signal readout. Rustrak recorders are handled by most of the larger electronics parts distributors. They are not sold directly to the public.

Connecting the Antenna to the Receiver

The first thing to do is to get the antenna hooked up to the antenna input of the FM receiver. The antenna should be clear of all nearby obstacles and face due south. The transmission line should be RG8/U and run as directly as possible to your receiver.

The termination impedance of the quad antenna is 75 ohms, so it will match properly with most FM receiver antenna-input terminals. On the other hand, if the receiver you use has a 300-ohm antenna input impedance, you will have to obtain a 75/300-ohm matching transformer. These are available from most electronics supply houses.

EFFECT OF INTEGRATION ON DETECTOR OUTPUT SIGNAL

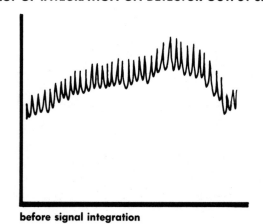

before signal integration

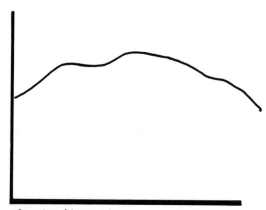

after signal integration

DETECTOR/INTEGRATOR CIRCUIT DIAGRAM

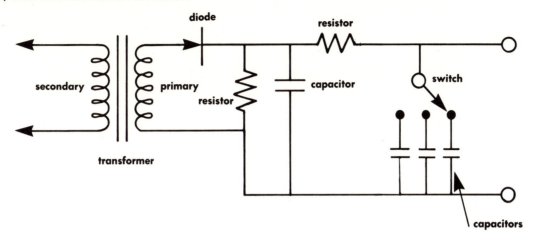

The secondary winding of the transformer is connected to the speaker terminals of the FM receiver. A standard 6.3-volt filament transformer is used to step up the low-impedance output from the receiver's audio system to a higher impedance for application to the diode detector stage.

Detector and Integrator

The signal voltage developed across the secondary winding of the transformer is applied to the diode detector stage. The output from the rectifier is a varying DC voltage, where amplitude is proportional to the received signal input. The output from the detector stage is applied to the integrator.

Now into Operation

Connect your signal readout meter or strip chart recorder to the output terminals. Be sure to observe proper polarity. Switch on the FM receiver and allow it to warm up for about 30 minutes. Adjust its gain control for midscale indication on the readout. If the receiver has tone controls, set them for a "flat" frequency response at the center of control rotation.

Connect your antenna and place the calibrator switch in the *calibrate* position. Adjust the volume control if necessary to obtain a half-full-scale reading. Next place the calibrator switch in the *antenna* position. If the system is working properly, you should note a slight increase in readout due to reception of cosmic radio noise. If you receive this "noise" you can be fairly sure that your telescope is operational.

A good test for the performance of your telescope is the detection of the large extended signal radiating from the center of the Milky Way. The thousands of radio stars in the area provide an intense combined signal that is detected on even the simplest telescope. The received signal appears as a curve extending over a number of hours.

Receiving the Sun

The next test for your telescope is the reception of solar radiation. Begin your observations for the sun at about 10:00 A.M. If you are using a voltmeter for your readout, take readings about every 10–15 minutes. If you are using a strip chart recorder, you can check it for any changes in reading.

As you approach 11:30, your readout device should begin to register an increase in received signal. At 12:00, when your antenna's beam is centered right at the sun, you should get the maximum reading. As the time passes to 1:00 P.M., the received sig-

RECORDING OF SOLAR RADIO SIGNALS

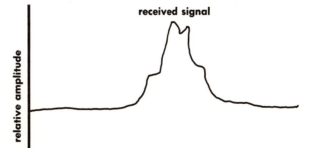

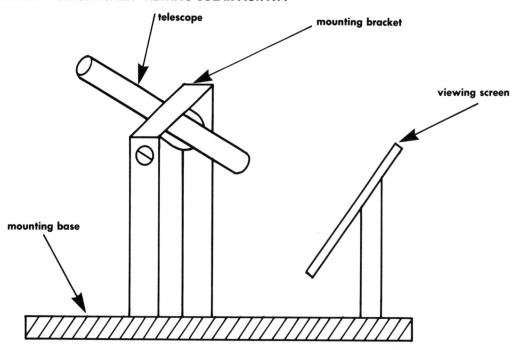

AN ARRANGEMENT FOR OPTICALLY VIEWING SOLAR ACTIVITY

nal level will drop. The overall curve should look like the one shown in the accompanying illustration.

The signals radiated from a "quiet" sun are much smaller than those from a "disturbed" sun. As you make day-to-day measurements, you will notice that the signals vary from a very slight increase in the received signal to "off-scale" readings when the sun is in its disturbed state. This continual change in solar activity is what makes observation of the sun so interesting.

Since most major solar radio activity coincides with the appearance of sunspots, you can "double your pleasure" by setting up a simple optical viewer. The Edmond Scientific Company makes a viewing telescope that can be mounted to focus the sun's image on a piece of cardboard. *You of course know not to view the sun directly!* With this arrangement you can correlate optical solar activity with its radio signal counterpart.

INDIRECT SOLAR TELESCOPE

Unlike the direct-reading telescope, this indirect unit operates at the VLF (very low frequency) end of the radio spectrum. VLF frequencies are those extending from about 16 KHz to 60 KHz. The lower part of the VLF band lies just above the audio frequency band.

The theory of operation of this telescope is as follows. During any 24-hour period there are thunderstorms occurring continually, particularly in the tropics. The "static" produced by these electrical storms seems to peak between 27 and 30 KHz. Under normal conditions the radio signals generated by these electrical storms stay near their origin. However, when a solar flare occurs, the ionospheric D-layer (the layer closest to the earth's surface) becomes ionized by intense ultraviolet and solar-particle radiation. This sudden "enhancement" of the D-layer causes the storm radio noise to be propagated around the globe to your receiving antenna. Putting it another way, the enhanced D-layer is an electrical conductor of the thunderstorm static to your receiving antenna.

There are several methods of detecting these signals, but perhaps the best approach is to use a frequency converter that will change the VLF signals to a higher frequency, which can then be tuned in on a regular communication receiver.

One of these units is manufactured by Polomar Engineers. This unit has an input frequency range of 10–500 KHz and a corresponding output frequency of 4,000–4,500 KHz. This converter has a

Observing the Sun

frequency that can be picked up by any shortwave receiver that will tune 4,000–4,500 KHz. If you don't happen to have one of these receivers on hand, perhaps you can borrow one from a ham radio operator. You can purchase a satisfactory receiver new for under $100.

The accompanying illustration shows the hookup for the VLF converter. The antenna is connected to the input terminal on the converter, while the converter's output terminals go to the communication receiver's antenna input terminals. The speaker terminals of the receiver are connected to the input of the detector/integrator.

The Antenna

The antenna for the VLF converter should be as long as possible because of the extremely low frequencies involved. I use a long wire antenna, about 60 feet in length. It is essential that an outside antenna be used. Any form of indoor antenna will be unsatisfactory. The reason for this is that harmonic frequencies from the 60-Hz household wiring will be received by the converter.

When you tune up your converter, try to find a clear frequency in the range between 25 and 30 KHz. Depending on your location, there may be interfering signals in this frequency range, so tune around to find a clear spot. What you want to receive (during the day) is a relatively constant background noise of fairly low level.

The accompanying illustration shows the type of signal response you should receive from your unit. Notice that, during daylight hours, the average signal level is low and increases at night. When a solar flare occurs, the ionosphere becomes conductive, or enhanced, and the noise level may equal or exceed the normal nighttime level.

A 144-MHz INTERFEROMETER

If you have at least 100 feet of clear space in your yard pointing in a southerly direction, you can assemble an excellent 144-MHz interferometer using two of the 7-element quad antennas described earlier. The increased gain and narrow beamwidth of this interferometer will allow you to get a stronger solar signal and to receive a number of discrete sources in the Milky Way, as well as many of the stronger radio sources in other galaxies.

All that is needed is the addition of a second 7-element quad antenna. The two antennas are spaced at least 100 feet apart and connected together by a length of 75-ohm (RG8/U) coaxial cable. At the *exact center* of the cable, a tee coaxial fitting is placed, and a length of cable is run from this point to your receiver input terminals.

Setup and operation of the interferometer are the same as for the single antenna radiometer, so I won't repeat the procedure again. The only difference will be the output signal, which will have a fan-shaped pattern.

COMPONENT ARRANGEMENT OF AN INDIRECT SOLAR FLARE RECEIVER

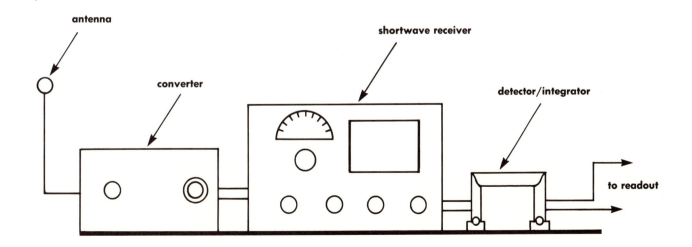

RECORDING OF A SOLAR BURST

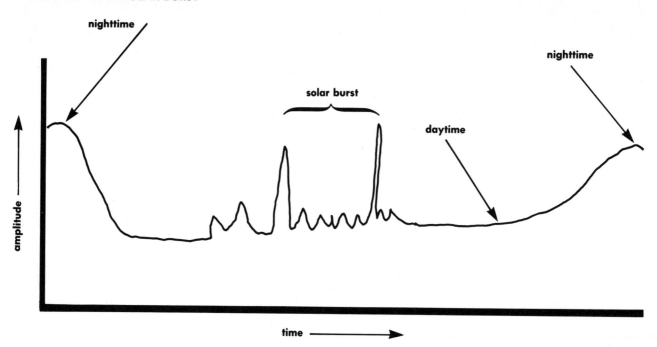

12 A 400-MHz Interferometer

There are many times when the amateur radio astronomer does not have a great deal of space available for the erection of an interferometer radio telescope. For example, the 144-MHz telescope described in the last chapter requires at least 100 feet between the antennas. The 400-MHz interferometer described in this chapter can help solve this problem, as it requires less spacing between the two antennas. Remember, for interferometer spacing, the higher the receiving frequency, the less distance required between antennas. As a result, this 400-MHz radio telescope will require only a 25-foot separation for the same resolution as the 144-MHz unit.

SYSTEM COMPONENTS

The accompanying block diagram shows the component arrangement of the 400-MHz radio telescope. As you can see, we are employing individual components or modules rather than an FM receiver, as was the case with the 108-MHz radiometer.

There are several reasons for using this modular approach. First, there are no FM receivers on the market that will receive 400 MHz. Second, inexpensive individual component modules are available to make construction easy.

The Antennas

While there are several approaches to the 400-MHz antennas, I recommend the use of a commercial amateur radio antenna for several reasons. First, at 400 MHz, antenna dimensions are critical and difficult to adjust. Second, the commercial antennas are mass produced and can be purchased for less money than you would spend on parts to build one yourself.

The antenna should have at least 15 elements and should have a minimum gain of 16 decibels at 400 MHz. There are several such antennas manufactured commercially, with a driven-element impedance of 75 ohms; these can be used directly with 75-ohm coaxial cable.

Signal Losses at 400 MHz

As the receiving frequency goes up, so do the signal losses because of increased leakage in the dielectric of the coaxial cable, insulators, connectors, etc. As a result, be sure not to skimp on the quality of the cable, connectors, and so on. I strongly suggest that you do not use solderless connectors, because their center connector pin can work loose from the coaxial cable's center conductor. Also, it is not possible to make a connection to the cable's outer shield braid with solderless connectors.

While there are several methods of mounting the two antennas, the use of two stepladders as mentioned earlier will be satisfactory because of the light weight of the antennas. In addition, the use of stepladders makes it easy to change the antenna spacing if desired.

Connecting the Antennas to the Receiver

As in the case of the 108-MHz interferometer, the two antennas are connected by a length of coaxial cable, the *exact* center of which is connected to a tee coaxial fitting. From the tee fitting, a second length of coaxial cable runs to the receiver's input terminals.

The length of the coaxial cable should be as short and direct as possible between the antenna tee connectors and the receiver's antenna input terminals. (Remember, the signal losses are greater at the higher frequencies.) *Use only RG8/U low-loss cable for this installation—do not use RG/58, etc.*

A 400-MHz INTERFEROMETER

antennas → calibration switch → RF amplifier → mixer oscillator → IF amplifier → detector/integrator → to readout

Receiver Component Interconnection

Individual modules are employed for the RF amplifier, converter, IF amplifier, and detector/integrator stages. The hookup of these modules is simple, and the manufacturer of each unit gives detailed installation information.

The detector/integrator is the same as the one described earlier. The input to the detector/integrator is connected to the output from the IF amplifier module, and the output from the detector/integrator is connected to the readout device.

The Power Supply

It is essential that a regulated power supply be used to provide operating power for the modules. The power supply should have an output voltage rating of 12 volts and a current rating of at least 1 ampere. These regulated power supplies can be obtained from such sources as Radio Shack or Olson Electronics, and they are not very expensive.

OPERATION

The basic operation of this 400-MHz telescope is the same as for the previously described 108-MHz unit. First, apply operating power to the modules and allow about 30 minutes for them to stabilize. Next, place the calibration reference switch in the *calibrate* position and note the reading. Now switch to the *antenna* position and again note the readout. If all is well, an increase in the reading should occur due to general background radiation. It should be noted that the *level* of this signal will be less at 400 MHz than at 108 MHz.

Let us take a moment to discuss antenna positioning. In the case of optical astronomy, it's important to accurately track the observed extraterrestrial source as it travels across the sky. As a result, optical telescopes are generally fitted with an equatorial mounting arrangement and often a clock drive.

In radio astronomy, the receiving antennas are fixed in position and receive signals as radio sources drift past the antenna with the earth's rotation. This is why they are referred to as drift radiometers, or drift interferometers. An example of this is the Arecibo antenna, which is obviously fixed in position. (This antenna does have provisions for slight shifts in effective elevation by adjusting the phase of the feed horns.) As far as the amateur radio telescope antenna is concerned, provisions for slight changes in elevation for solar observations are all that is required.

13 Receiving Signals from Jupiter

The planet Jupiter, in conjunction with its moon Io, produces very intense radio emission. These signals occur in the frequency range of 18–22 MHz, in contrast to other stellar radio signals, which lie in the VHF and UHF regions.

Unlike "conventional" extraterrestrial radio signals, the Jovian signals resemble the sound of rushing surf or distant thunderstorms. As a result, they are most interesting to listen to, and many radio astronomers tape record them for future playback. This is one case where a strip chart recorder is not necessary for signal readout.

RECEIVING JOVIAN-IO SIGNALS

As shown in the accompanying illustration, the Jovian radio telescope system consists of an antenna and a shortwave receiver. A detector/integrator is not needed, as we are interested in the audio signal. As a result, the communication receiver's speaker serves as the "readout" device.

The Antenna

There are several possible approaches to making the antenna for the Jupiter receiver. If you are in an area of fairly low terrestrial radio noise, the resonant half-wave dipole will be satisfactory if you have a reasonably good receiver. The accompanying illlustration shows the construction of the dipole antenna. It is designed to be resonant at 22 MHz. The end supports for this antenna can be two trees, your house and a tree, or whatever. The termination impedance of the antenna is 75 ohms, so you can use standard RG8/U coaxial cable for connection to the receiver.

BASIC JUPITER-IO SIGNAL RECEIVER

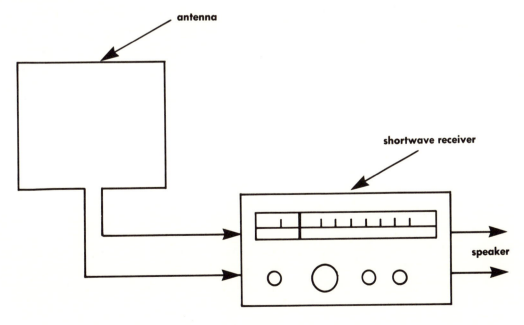

DIPOLE ANTENNA FOR JUPITER-IO RECEIVER

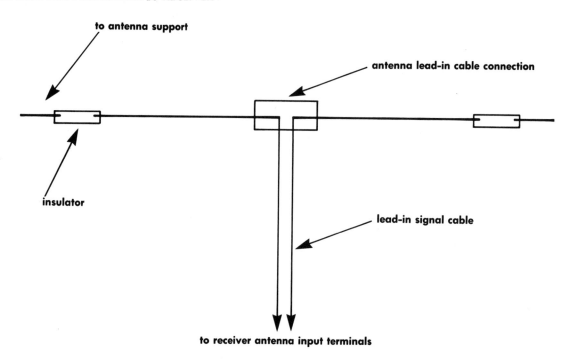

Since Jupiter travels in an east-west direction, the ends of the dipole should be pointed north-south. This will provide maximum signal input to the antenna. (Remember, maximum signal pickup occurs when a dipole is perpendicular to the radiated signal pattern.)

The Receiver

Any reasonably sensitive shortwave receiver capable of tuning between 20 and 24 MHz (15–13 meters) will be satisfactory. If you wish to purchase a receiver, check sources such as Radio Shack and receiver manufacturers listed in *Q.S.T.* or *C.Q.* magazines. The classified sections of these magazines often list good deals on used receivers. Failing these approaches, a ham radio friend may loan you his receiver.

Receiver Selectivity

Concerning extraterrestrial radio signals in the VHF and UHF frequencies, it is desirable to have as wide a receiver bandpass as possible in order to receive the maximum signal power.

In the case of a receiver for Jupiter signals, just the reverse is true. Because of the large number of terrestrial radio signals in the 20–24 MHz range, it is essential that the Jupiter signal receiver have a narrow bandpass in order to be able to separate out the Jovian signals.

To receive the Jupiter signals, you must first determine when Jupiter appears in the sky over your antenna. *Sky and Telescope* and *Astronomy* magazines give monthly star and planet reports to help you locate the various planets. Since Jupiter is a bright object in the sky, you can easily spot it. Due to the wide beamwidth of the dipole, 180°, it will "see" Jupiter during its entire trip across the sky. As a result, if you can see Jupiter, so will the antenna.

Tuning in the Signal

Once you have located Jupiter, the next step is to tune your receiver in the range of 20–22 MHz. The signal that you are looking for will have the sound of rushing surf, or sometimes it will sound like distant thunder. I might mention that Jupiter does not always cooperate. There may be several days or more when it will emit no signals. Once you begin listening to the Jupiter signals, you may want to record them. The recorded sounds make a great conversation piece.

Receiving Signals from Jupiter

THE LOOP ANTENNA

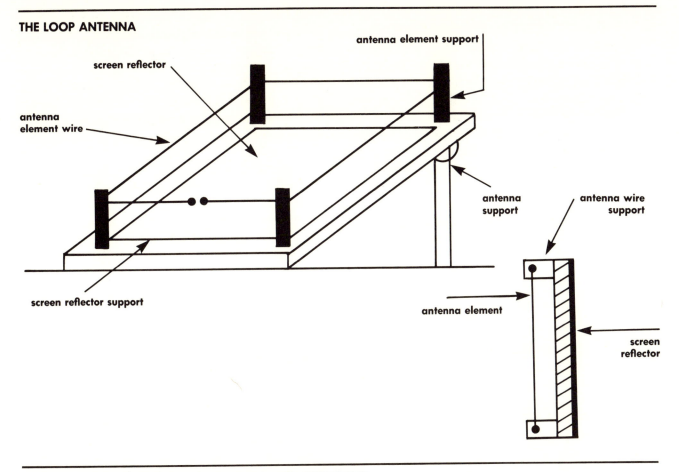

ADDING A PREAMPLIFIER TO INCREASE RECEIVER SENSITIVITY

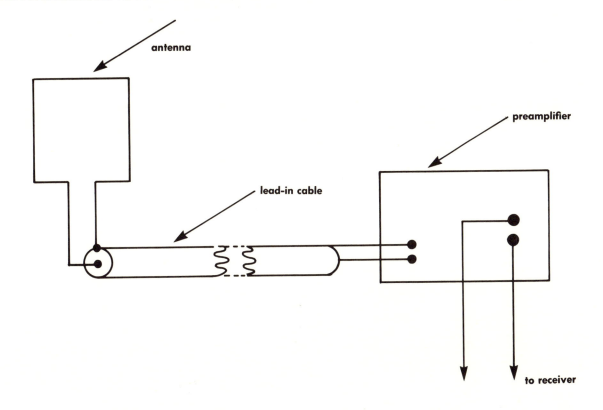

A BETTER ANTENNA

If you live in a fairly noisy location, the antenna shown in the accompanying illustration should be helpful. This antenna has a narrower beamwidth than the simple dipole just described and will tune out some of the terrestrial interference.

The antenna's driven element consists of a square loop of wire, one-eighth wavelength per side at 22 MHz. This dimension is calculated as follows:

$$\text{Wavelength} = \frac{300}{\text{Frequency (in MHz)}}$$
$$= \frac{300}{22} = 13.6 \text{ meters}$$
$$= 13.6 \times 0.125 = 1.7 \text{ meters}$$
$$= 1.7 \times 3.28 = 5.5 \text{ feet}$$

Thus, each side of the driven element is 5.5 feet long. For the driven element wire, use solid aluminum clothesline wire, which is available at a local hardware store. If you can't find this, a suitable substitution is #4 or #6 aluminum TV guy wire, which can be obtained at most electronics parts supply houses.

The frame for the antenna is made up from four 6-foot-long pieces of 1-inch-x-2-inch pine. When you purchase the wood be sure that the pieces are straight and free of knots. Most lumber is actually shy of the stated dimensions, so the wood you get will probably be ⅞ inches x 1⅞ inches. This is no problem.

The driven element is backed up with a screen reflector spaced 12 inches behind the driven element. While this is not the optimum spacing, it is satisfactory. A center brace in the reflector frame helps to support the screen.

The free ends of the driven element loop are connected to a piece of plastic into which two 6/32-inch-x-1-inch *brass* machine screws and nuts are inserted. These screws serve as the terminals for the driven element.

The antenna is simply rested on the ground and propped up by a wooden stick. Antenna elevation is accomplished simply by changing the stick's angle.

This antenna has a directional receiving pattern. Therefore it is necessary to aim the antenna at Jupiter for maximum signal pickup. Although this antenna has a narrower beamwidth than the dipole, it is still wide enough so you don't have to track Jupiter exactly "on the nose" as with an optical telescope.

Adding a Preamplifier

If you are having difficulty receiving the Jupiter signals, it may be that the receiver lacks sufficient sensitivity. You can solve this problem by adding an RF signal preamplifier between the antenna and the receiver input. This preamplifier should have a relatively flat frequency response over the 20–24-MHz frequency range.

The accompanying illustration shows a typical hookup for the RF preamplifier. The antenna lead-in is connected to the antenna terminals of the RF amplifier. A shielded lead is connected from the output terminals of the RF preamplifier to the antenna terminals of the receiver.

14 Detection of Meteors and Meteor Showers

Investigation of meteors and their trails is of considerable interest to the radio astronomer, as these meteors can yield much information about the nature of the universe. From the terrestrial point of view, meteors and meteor showers have a direct effect on long-distance VHF and UHF terrestrial radio communications.

On a clear, moonless night, you can generally spot an occasional "shooting star," or meteor. The naked eye can generally spot from 2 to 15 meteors per hour, depending on the time of night and the season of the year. At certain times during the year the number of visible meteors will increase to as many as 100–200 per hour. This large number of simultaneous meteors is known as a *meteor shower*, and it appears to come from a single point in the sky, known as the *radiant* of the shower. While these meteors appear to move outward from a single point in space, actually they travel on parallel courses. It is the viewer's perspective that makes them appear to originate from a point source.

The meteors that you are able to observe are only a very small portion of the actual number of meteors striking the earth's atmosphere. There are several reasons for this. First, your eyes can observe only a small portion of the heavens at one time. Second, your eyes are sensitive only to the brighter meteors. There are many more that are too faint to be seen by the unaided eye. In fact, it has been estimated that 500 million meteors enter our atmosphere every day.

As the meteor enters the earth's atmosphere, it becomes heated by air resistance. Eventually, it becomes heated to the point of incandescence, and this is when we see it. As the meteor travels still further into an increasingly dense atmosphere, it begins to leave a trail of ionized particles, mainly electrons stripped from their atoms by the intense heat. As the meteor nears the surface of the earth, it will probably be completely disintegrated by the intense heat of friction. A few of the larger meteors will not be completely disintegrated, however, and will reach the surface of the earth as *meteorites*.

One of the major difficulties in observing meteors is that it is impossible to observe them visually during daylight hours. This problem is solved by using radio techniques to observe and count meteors and meteor-scattering events.

RADAR METHODS

As we have mentioned, the superheated meteors leave a trail of ionized particles, which are electrically conductive. As a result, a radar signal directed at these ionized particles will be reflected back to the radar receiver. The radar echoes are recorded on a cathode-ray tube and can be counted.

The frequency range used in these radar systems is above the critical frequency of the ionosphere (above 18 MHz) and may range as high as 100 MHz. Extraterrestrial signals below the critical frequency are absorbed by the ionosphere, and the critical frequency will vary slightly from day to day.

SIGNAL REFLECTION METHOD

Another method of detecting meteors makes use of a commercial radio broadcasting station in conjunction with a standard FM receiver. The FM receiver is tuned to an FM broadcasting station that is located over the earth's horizon. Since the FM station's signal is VHF, it will travel skyward, rather than follow the curvature of the earth. But a meteor shower will act as an artificial "ionosphere," bending the transmitter's signal around the curvature of the earth to the receiver. The amount of signal re-

INDIRECT METHOD OF METEOR DETECTION

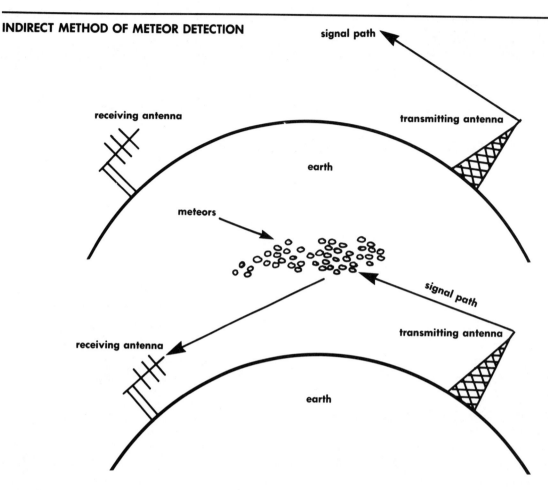

turned to the receiver will depend on the number of meteors.

Audio Monitoring

There are several signal readout methods that are appropriate for use in meteor detection, but one of the simplest involves the use of a tape recorder connected to the output of the receiver tuned to the distant station. A long-playing cassette or a reel-to-reel recorder is connected to the receiver, and the recorder is left in the record position for a number of hours.

To check the results, rather than setting the recorder in the normal playback mode, set it in the fast-forward mode. When any sounds are detected, stop the recorder, then reverse it for a few feet of tape. Then switch the recorder to the play mode and identify the signals. This approach is better than listening to the whole tape at the slow play mode, since it is possible that two hours might pass before any signals are detected.

Since the FM signal being received is over the horizon, you will hear no signal until meteors come between your receiver and FM transmitter. When a meteor does come between, you will receive a burst of signal, its intensity and duration depending on the number of meteors.

Locating a Station

Since the FM station you want to monitor is over the horizon, you can't normally receive it. As a result, you can use a publication such as the *World Radio Atlas* to locate an appropriate station. There are also other publications that list commercial FM stations, including the *FM Atlas*, available from Bruce Eberling, P.O. Box 24, Adolf, MN 55701.

A PRACTICAL METEOR SHOWER RECEIVER

Now that we have examined the principles and system requirements for a meteor shower radio telescope, let's build one. The telescope consists of an

Detection of Meteors and Meteor Showers

SETUP FOR TAPE RECORDING METEORS

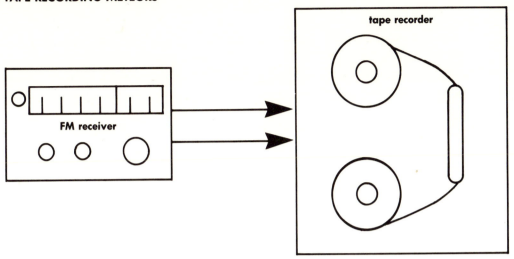

antenna, FM receiver, audio tape recorder, detector/integrator, and chart recorder if desired.

The Antenna

When you are using a commercial FM broadcasting station as the signal source, you must use a high-gain, narrow-beamwidth antenna. There are several reasons for this. First, the desired FM station will be over the horizon, so the only signals received will be those reflected by the meteor shower. These returned signals will be very low in amplitude, several microvolts or less, so a high-gain antenna is necessary. Second, because of the many commercial FM stations in operation, a highly directive antenna is a necessity in order to separate the desired station from the stronger local FM stations. Generally, a high-gain beam antenna is used. Several manufacturers produce so-called long-distance FM receiving antennas that will be satisfactory.

If you wish, you can use the 7-element quad antenna described earlier. I recommend the use of the quad, as it has a gain of about 14 decibels and has a relatively narrow beamwidth. Also, the quad has a bit better front-to-back ratio than a corresponding beam antenna. The virtue of this is that interfering signals at the back of the antenna will not be received.

I suggest the use of a TV-type antenna rotor so that the antenna can be focused on the desired distant station. Since the antenna is lightweight, an inexpensive rotor can be used.

The connections between the antenna should be made with low-loss transmission line such as RG8/U coaxial cable. Additionally, the cable fittings should be soldered, rather than the solderless type.

The Receiver

Since we are dealing with very weak signals, a reasonably high-quality FM receiver should be used, with an input of 2 decibels for 10-decibel quieting, or better. The better receiver manufacturers will list their input sensitivity in their specs. As a matter of reference, a receiver with a 2-decibel-for-10-decibel quieting will provide more signal for less internally generated noise than one with, say, a 6-decibel-for-10-decibel quieting. It's just a matter of the *usable* receiver signal sensitivity.

If your FM receiver lacks sufficient sensitivity, it may be necessary to add an external RF signal preamplifier to boost the received signals before they are applied to the FM receiver. There are a number of commercial FM RF preamplifiers, or "boosters," as they are sometimes called, on the market.

15 Some Final Words

We are going to give some tips and thoughts that should enhance your enjoyment of your amateur radio astronomy hobby.

THREE IS NOT A CROWD

Some of the projects described here require a fair amount of equipment, often more than one experimenter may have in his junk box. So sometimes it's a good idea to team up with several other people who can help contribute the equipment required to build the project. For example, one person may have a good receiver and components for a radio telescope project but no antenna, while a friend may have a good 140-MHz amateur radio beam antenna that could be donated to the project. Still a third friend may have access to a strip chart recorder that could be used to complete the project.

If you are not an amateur radio operator, you may have a friend who is. Mention your project to him and he may be willing to help out.

Still another source is the physics or electrical engineering department of your local college or university. You will be surprised how much help they can offer if you explain your project. Often, they can loan equipment, such as a strip chart recorder, on a limited basis.

CLUBS

With the increased interest in amateur radio astronomy, there are a number of local amateur radio astronomy clubs sprouting up around the U.S. Often, these groups are tied in with optical astronomy clubs, so you might check with your local optical astronomy club on this. There is also a national amateur radio astronomy organization: Society of Amateur Radio Astronomers (SARA), 1548 Bell Flower Court, Stone Mountain, GA 30058. They publish a newsletter as well as other information.

Following are some hints and suggestions that will be helpful in the operation and troubleshooting of your radio telescope.

COMPENSATING FOR RECEIVER NOISE

The signal applied to the readout device, a strip chart or meter, consists of two components. The first component, which remains constant, is the noise generated by the receiver, transmission lines, etc., and the second component is the desired signal. If suitable means are not provided, the noise will mask the desired signal. To compensate for this, an offset voltage is applied to the readout device in a manner to "buck out" the receiver noise signal, leaving only the desired extraterrestrial signal.

One method of providing this compensation is shown in the accompanying illustration. The control circuit consists of a 3-volt battery (two 1½-volt cells in series), a potentiometer, and isolating resistors.

CHECKING RECEIVER DRIFT

One of the problems often overlooked is that of long-term receiver drift. Often it will appear that an increase or decrease in received signal is being observed, when actually the variation is being caused by drift on the receiver. Obviously, any such drift will provide erroneous readings.

To check for receiver drift, connect a resistor of the same resistance value as the antenna input impedance of your receiver across the input terminals.

EFFECT OF RECEIVER NOISE LEVEL ON READOUT

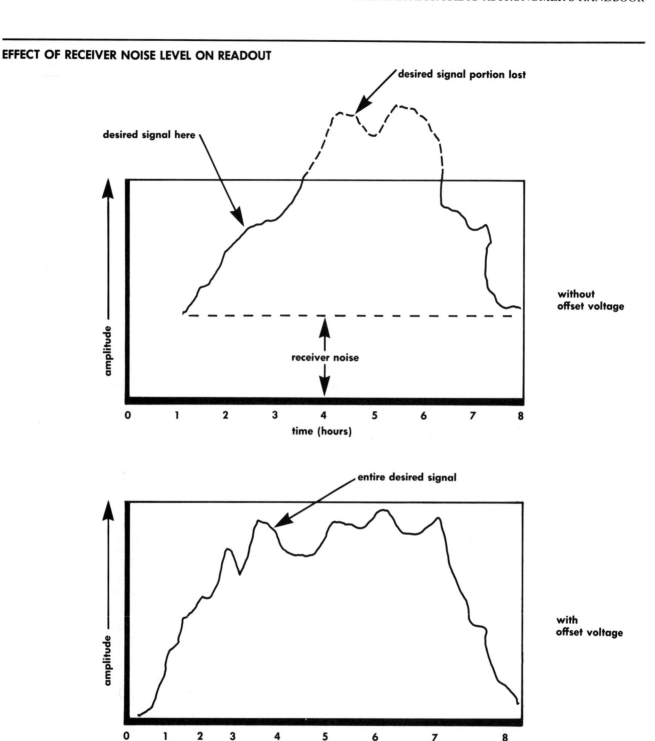

Next, with the readout meter or chart recorder set for a convenient reading, allow the receiver to run for 24 hours. By observing the readout at the end of this 24-hour period, you can note any variation in receiver output. Then, when you are taking actual signal measurements, this receiver drift can be noted and compensated for.

Cures for Receiver Drift

There are several things that can be done to cure, or at least reduce, receiver drift. Almost every receiver or converter employs a local oscillator to provide the heterodyne frequency conversion process. Any drift in this local oscillator's operating fre-

Some Final Words

RECEIVER-NOISE OFFSET CONTROL SCHEMATIC

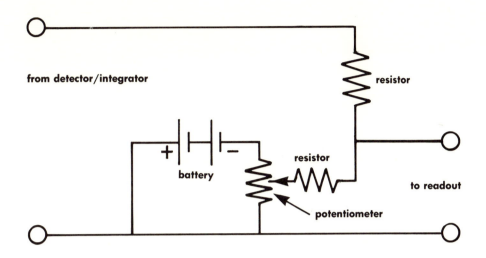

ARRANGEMENT FOR CHECKING TRANSMISSION LINE NOISE

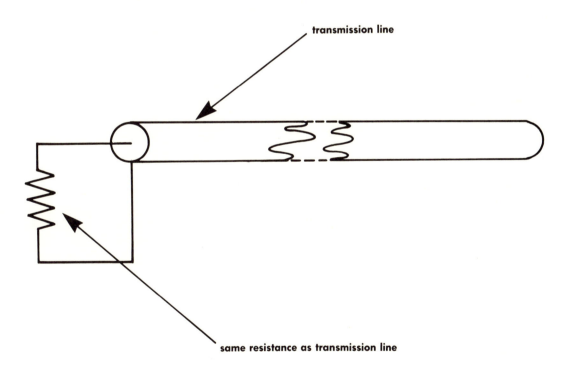

quency will be reflected as a corresponding drift in the receiver's output signal. In turn, the local oscillator's frequency is, to a point, a function of its supply voltage, so regulating its supply voltage will tend to stabilize it. A Zenor diode voltage regulator can be placed in the DC voltage supply to the local oscillator to stabilize its operating voltage.

Line Voltage Variations

Another cause of receiver drift is variation in the line voltage. As we all know, the 120-volt supply voltage does not remain constant but will vary during periods of the day and night. Also, switching on and off appliances, such as an electric iron or stove,

THIS DECOUPLING NETWORK WILL PREVENT COMMON POWER SUPPLY CIRCUIT OSCILLATIONS

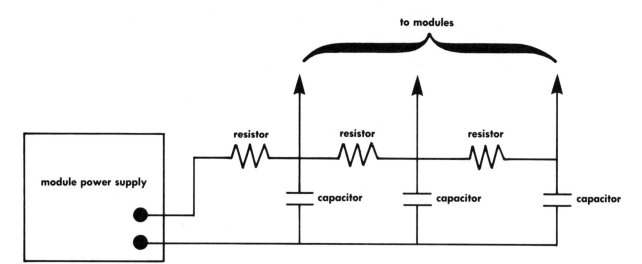

in the house will vary the line voltage.

One solution to this problem is the use of a so-called *constant voltage transformer*. These constant voltage transformers are available at most electrical supply houses at reasonable cost.

TRANSMISSION LINE NOISE

One of the points often overlooked is that of transmission line noise. Often, it will appear that an extraterrestrial signal is being received when the receiver calibration switch is placed in the *antenna* position. This increase in received noise is partly the actual extraterrestrial signal and partly transmission line noise.

There is a method to differentiate between the actual extraterrestrial signal and transmission line noise. The transmission line is disconnected from the antenna, a resistor of the same resistance as the line impedance (75 or 300 ohms) is temporarily connected across the ends of the line, and the detector/integrator's output voltage is recorded.

Next, remove the resistor from the ends of the line and connect the line back to the antenna, and again note the signal output reading. There should be a significant difference in the readings. If there is not, either your antenna is not receiving any signals, or you have an excessively leaky transmission line. Also, check your RF connectors for poor connections.

TROUBLESHOOTING

The following troubleshooting tips may be useful if you are having difficulty getting your telescope to operate properly.

You may have a condition where you get a large output voltage from your detector/integrator, even with no input signal. This condition, which is the result of overall system feedback, or oscillation, most often occurs in a modular arrangement. The problem is caused by a common signal voltage being developed on the common power supply voltage source.

The cure for this problem is to use decoupling capacitors and decoupling resistors in the DC supply line feeding the various modules. The component values are not critical. A 20% tolerance is acceptable.

Module Shielding

Uninvited circuit oscillations can occur if the individual modules are not properly shielded from each other. One method of shielding the individual modules involves mounting each module in a mini-box metal enclosure. These enclosures are available in a number of sizes and shapes from various manufacturers, such as Bud Radio and Radio Shack. The module's printed circuit boards should be mounted away from the metal bottom of the box by means of small spacers. DC operating power and input and

Some Final Words 99

THIS TRAP WILL FILTER OUT AN UNWANTED FM SIGNAL

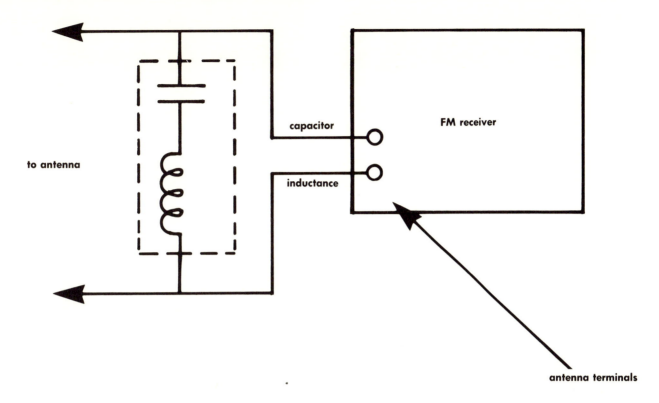

output RF connections are brought out to connectors outside the box.

System Grounding

It is very important that a good earth ground be provided for the complete radio telescope. The best ground is the *cold* water pipe. If this is not available, a copper ground rod driven into the ground will do the trick. Also, be sure to employ a large diameter #12 or #10 stranded wire for the grounding.

Local Station Interference

If you are using an FM receiver for your radio telescope, you may experience interference from a local FM station, even though you have tuned outside the actual FM band. This effect is especially prevalent on inexpensive FM receivers that don't have sufficient front-end selectivity. Also, if there is a high-power FM station nearby, an effect known as *cross-modulation* may occur, so that you will hear that particular station over almost the entire tuning dial.

One solution to this problem is the installation of a "trap" to filter out the interfering station. This consists of a series-tuned resonant circuit connected directly across the antenna terminals of the FM receiver. The values of the capacitor and the inductance are chosen to be resonant at the frequency of the offending FM station.

To determine the correct values for these two components, the following formula is used:

$$F = \frac{10^6}{2\pi\sqrt{LC}}$$

where: F = frequency in KHz
L = inductance in microhenries
C = capacitance in picofarads
π = 3.14

In extreme cases, it may be necessary to enclose the filter in a small metal box that is properly grounded.

Using the Milky Way for Calibration

The extended radio source from the galactic plane of our Milky Way makes an excellent calibration source for the amateur radio telescope. The net power of this extended radio source remains constant, never varying from day to day, as does solar radiation. The received signal is in the form of a nice, rounded curve with a total duration of about 6 hours. The beauty of this method of calibration is that it can be used as a performance check for the entire radio telescope system: antennas, RF preamplifier/mixer, IF amplifier, detector/integrator, and readout device. If your telescope shows a consistent Milky Way signal, day in and day out, your set is in good shape.

Index

Amplifiers, 68–71, 86
Antennas
   Arecibo, 86
   beam, 73
   cable connectors and, 60
   collinear, 56–57, *56*, 69
   corner reflector, 57, *57*
   coupling to receivers, 58, 60, 80–81, 85–86
   design and construction of, 73–77
   in Dicke system, 47
   directors and, 55–56, *55*
   dish, 58, *58, 59*
   folded dipole, 55
   4-bay quad, 75, *75*
   400-MHz interferometer and, 85
   gain requirements, 68–69
   general properties of, 51–53
   half-wave dipole, 87–88
   helical, 69, 75–76, *76*
   Jupiter and, 87–90, *88, 89*
   Kraus, 46, *46*
   loop, 89, *90*
   meteor detection and, 93
   Mills Cross, 44–46, *46*
   mounting of, 60, 76
   1,000 foot Arecibo, *48, 49*
   parabolic, 58, *58, 59*
   paraboloid, 57, *57*
   positioning of, 86
   quad, 73–74, *74*
   space-age helical, 57, *58*
   sun and, 79–80, 83
   transmission lines and, 60
   two antenna interferometer, 41–43, *42, 43*
   types of radio telescope, 53–58
Aperture, 52
Arecibo antenna, 1,000 foot, *48, 49*, 86
Assembling a radio telescope, 62–72
   antennas, 73–77
   component requirements of, 68–70
   mechanical assembly of, 70–72, *71*
   modular approach, 69–70, *70*
   operating frequency of, 67
   operation and troubleshooting, 95–100
   power supplies, 71
   quad antenna, details for, 73–74
   selecting components for, 67–68
Astronomy magazine, 88
Audio monitoring of meteors, 92, *93*
Audio monitors, 66

Bandwidth, 52, *62*, 62, *64*, 64
Beam antenna, 73
Beamwidth, 42–43, *52*, 52, 55
Brightness temperature, 51

Cable connectors, 60
Calibration, *65, 66*, 99–100
Capacitors, 29–30, *29*
Cliff interferometer, 47, *49*
Clubs, radio astronomy, 95
Collinear antenna, 56–57, *56*, 69
Computers, 66
Constant voltage transformer, 98
Constructing a radio telescope.
   See Assembling a radio telescope

Corner reflector antenna, 57, *57*
Current, 27, 30–32, *32*

DC amplifier, 65
Detectors, 65, 81, *81*, 86
Dicke system, 47, *47*
Dipole antenna. *See* Folded dipole antenna; Half-wave dipole antenna
Directors, antenna and, 55–56, *55*
Discrete signal, 14
Dish antenna, 58, *58*, 59
Doppler effect, 11–12
Drift radiometer, 41

Electromagnetic spectrum, 5–7, *6*
Electronic circuits, 27, 30, *31*
Electronic noise, mixer-stage, 63
Electronics, 27–39. *See also specific topics*
Electronic symbols, 27, *28*
Extended signal, 14
Extraterrestrial radio sources, 13–18
 extended and discrete, 14, *14*
 galactic and extragalactic, 15
 hydrogen line, 15–16
 Jupiter, 17
 meteors, 17–18, *18*
 nonthermal synchrotron, 13–14
 the planets, 17
 signal attenuation, 11
 the sun, 16–17, *16*
 thermal and nonthermal, 13–14, *13*

Flux density, 51
FM Atlas, 92
FM broadcasting, 91–93, 99, *99*
Folded dipole antenna, 55
Forward gain, 52, 55
4-Bay quad antenna, 75, *75*
400-MHz interferometer, 85–86, *86*
Frequency, 5–7
Front-to-back ratio, 53

Galileo, 19
Grounding, 71, 99

Half-wave dipole antenna, 53–55, *55*, 58, 87–88
Helical antenna, 69, 75–76, *76*
Heterodyne oscillator, 63
Heterodyne process, 63

Impedance, 53
Inductance, 30, *30*
Integrators, 81, *81*, 86
 sun and, 80, *80*
 superheterodyne receiver and, 65, *65*
Interference, 99
Interferometers, 77
 Cliff, 47, *49*
 400-MHz, 85–86, *86*
 144-MHz interferometer, 83
 phase-switching, 43–44, *44*, *45*
 sun and, 83
 two-antenna, 41–43, *42*, *43*
Intermediate frequency (IF) amplifier, 64, *64*
Ionosphere, radio wave propagation and, 9–12, *10*, *11*

Jupiter, 14, 17, 66, 87–90
 antennas and, 87–90, *88*, *89*
 preamplifiers and, 90
 receivers and, 87, *88*

Kraus antenna, 46, *46*

Line voltage variations, 97–98
Loop antennas, 89, *90*

Meteors, detection of, 91–93, *92*, *93*
Meteor showers, 12, 17–18
Meteor trails, 17
Milky Way, 14–15, *14*, 43, 44, 68, 81, 83
 calibration using, 99–100
Mills Cross Antenna, 44–46, *46*
Module shielding, circuit oscillations and, 98–99, *98*

Index

Newton, Sir Isaac, 19

Ohm's law, 27, 53
1,000 foot Arecibo antenna, *48*, 49
Optical astronomy
  basics of, 19, 20–23, *23*, 24
  light measurement and, 51
  radio astronomy compared to, 5–8, *7*
  signal processing in, 24
  solar radio activity, 82, *82*
  star positions and, 23
Optical telescopes, 19, 20–23, *23*
  radio telescopes compared to, 7–8, *7*
Organic molecules, 15–16, *15*
Oscillators, receiver drift and, 96–97

Parabolic antenna, 58, *58*, *59*
Paraboloid antenna, 57, *57*
Parametric amplifier, 61–62
Phase-switching interferometer, 43–44, *44*, *45*
Plank's law, 51
Polarization, 53
Power, 27
Power line interference, 71, *71*
Power supplies, 37–38, *38*, 86, 98–99, *98*
Power supply filters, 39, *39*
Preamplifiers, 68, 90

Quad antenna, 73–74, *74*

Radiation, characteristics of received, 51
Radio astronomy. *See also specific topics*
  basic systems of, 41–49
  optical astronomy compared to, 5–8, *7*
Radio broadcasts, FM, 91–93, 99, *99*
Radio sources, extraterrestrial. *See* Extraterrestrial radio sources

Radio telescopes (radiometers), 41–49, *41*. *See also specific topics*
  assembly of home system, 67–72
  direct solar radio receiver, 79–81, *79*
  indirect solar, 82–83, *83*
  optical telescopes compared to, 7–8, *7*
  VLA (Very Large Array), 24–25
Radio waves, 9–12, *10*, *11*
Radio window, 13
Readout devices, 66, 80, 95, 96, 97
Receivers, 69
  cable connectors and, 60
  coupling antenna to, 58, 60
  coupling to the antenna, 80–81, 85–86
  electrical noise and, 61–62, *61*
  400-MHz interferometer and, 86
  Jupiter and, signals from, 87, 88
  meteor detection and, 93
  receiver drift and, 95–98
  receiver noise and, 95, 96, 97
  sun and, 80
  superheterodyne, 62–65, *63*
  transmission lines and, 60
  types of, 62
Reflector telescopes, 19, 54–55, *55*
Refractor telescopes, 19
Resistance, 27, 28, 53
Resistors, 28, *29*
Resolution, 23–25
Rich field telescope, 19

Schmidt-Cassegrain telescopes, 19
Semiconductors, 34, *35*
Signal processing, 24, *25*
Sky and Telescope magazine, 88
Society of Amateur Radio Astronomers (SARA), 95
Solar flares, 10–11, 16, 79
Solar storms, 10–11

Space age helical antenna, 57, *58*
Square law detector, 65
Stars, positions of, 23
Sudden ionospheric disturbance, 16
Sun, the, 16–17, *16*, 44, 77, 79–84
   antennas and, 79–80, 83
   direct solar radio receiver and, 79–81, *79*
   indirect solar telescope, 82–83, *83*
   integrators and, 80, *80*
   interferometers, 83
   readout devices and, 80
   receivers and, 80
   solar radiation, reception of, 81–82, *81*, 84
Sunspots, 10–11, 16, 82
Superheterodyne receiver, 62–65, *63*

Synchrotron radiation, nonthermal, 13–14

Termination, 53
Thermal agitation, 61
Tolerance, 28
Transformers, 32, *33*, 34
Transistors, 34–35, *36*, 37
Transmission lines, 60, 97, 98
Tropospheric refraction, 11
Tuned radio frequency receiver, 62
Two-antenna interferometer, 41–43, *42*, *43*

Voltage, 27, 97–98

Wavelength, 5–8, 42–43
World Radio Atlas, 92

X-ray astronomy, 7
X-rays, 6–7